# TEACHING INFORMATION LITERACY THROUGH SHORT STORIES

# TEACHING INFORMATION LITERACY THROUGH SHORT STORIES

## David J. Brier
## Vickery Kaye Lebbin

ROWMAN & LITTLEFIELD
Lanham • Boulder • New York • London

Published by Rowman & Littlefield
A wholly owned subsidiary of The Rowman & Littlefield Publishing Group,
Inc.
4501 Forbes Boulevard, Suite 200, Lanham, Maryland 20706
www.rowman.com

Unit A, Whitacre Mews, 26-34 Stannary Street, London SE11 4AB

British Library Cataloguing in Publication Information Available

**Library of Congress Cataloging-in-Publication Data**

Names: Brier, David James, 1962 author. | Lebbin, Vickery Kaye, 1969- author.
Title: Teaching information literacy through short stories / David James Brier, Vickery Kaye
    Lebbin.
Description: Lanham, Maryland : Rowman & Littlefield, 2016. | Includes bibliographical refer-
    ences.
Identifiers: LCCN 2016016862 (print) | LCCN 2016030911 (ebook) | ISBN 9781442255449
    (cloth : alk. paper) | ISBN 9781442255456 (pbk. : alk. paper) | ISBN 9781442255463 (elec-
    tronic)
Subjects: LCSH: Information literacy—Study and teaching (Secondary) | Short story.
Classification: LCC ZA3075 .B75 2016 (print) | LCC ZA3075 (ebook) | DDC 028.7071/2—dc23
LC record available at https://lccn.loc.gov/2016016862

Printed in the United States of America

# 94975016s

# CONTENTS

# PREFACE

This book developed from our ongoing search for new teaching methods to make information literacy meaningful for students. Several years ago, we discovered the following two books by history professor Daniel Roselle: *Transformations: Understanding World History through Science Fiction* (Fawcett, 1973) and *Transformations II: Understanding American History through Science Fiction* (Fawcett, 1974). Roselle's books include collections of short stories linked to various history topics. Thinking it would be fun to try this approach with information literacy, we found a few promising short stories and used them in several classes. The result was so positive that it led to a search through literary review journals, indexes, and anthologies for more short stories. In 2004, we presented this teaching strategy at the LOEX-of-the-West library instruction conference and wrote a paper included in a special issue of the journal *Reference Services Review* focused on the conference. Following the conference, we continued to collect more short stories with the goal of eventually sharing our collection with other teachers and librarians in a published anthology. Through the years we used the short stories in library workshops for various subject disciplines. We asked students to read the stories at different times—before, during, and after a workshop and to respond to discussion questions through assorted techniques—individually, as groups, in person, and online.

In January 2016 something opportune occurred. After several years of work and discussion by many librarians, the Association of College and Research Libraries (ACRL) adopted the *Framework for Informa-*

*tion Literacy for Higher Education*, the new guiding document for the development of information literacy programs within higher education. The *Framework* is a significant update and revision to the *Informational Literacy Competency Standards for Higher Education*. This new *Framework*, designed to encourage a deeper understanding of information literacy, provides an ideal structure for a collection of short stories that encourage richer discussions about information literacy. ACRL encouraged librarians to be imaginative and innovative in implementing the *Framework*. The timing was right for us to act on that suggestion and compile this anthology of short stories linked to the *Framework*. The stories in the books are categorized according to the six frames in the *Framework for Information Literacy for Higher Education*. We are grateful to the authors who wrote the short stories included in this book and the multitude of librarians who contributed to the *Framework* that provides the book's structure. It is through your work we are able to present to teachers, instructors, and librarians what we hope is a fun and worthwhile text for teaching and exploring information literacy.

# ACKNOWLEDGMENTS

Framework for Information Literacy for Higher Education," American Library Association, February 9, 2015. http://www.ala.org/acrl/standards/ilframework. Reprinted by permission of the Association of College and Research Libraries.

"Renaissance Man" by T. E. D. Klein. Copyright © 1974 Abelard-Schuman, 450 Edgeware Road, London W2. Originally published in *Space 2*, edited by Richard Davis. Reprinted by permission of the author.

"The Liberation of Rome" by Robin Hemley. Originally appeared in *North Carolina Humanities* and *The Big Ear: Stories by Robin Hemley*. Copyright © 1995 Robin Hemley. Reprinted by permission of the author.

"The Amphibious Cavalry Gap" by James E. Thompson. Copyright © 1974 Conde Nast Publications, Inc. First printed in *Analog Science Fiction and Fact*, February 1974, and reprinted by permission of Penny Publications LLC/Dell Magazines.

"Megaphone" by Rick Cook. Copyright © 1988 Baen Publishing Enterprises. Originally appeared in *New Destinies: The Paperback Magazine of Science Fiction and Speculative Fact 6* (1988): 217–24. Reprinted by permission of the author.

"The Voice from the Curious Cube" by Nelson Bond. Copyright © 1937, 1954 Nelson Bond. Reprinted by permission of the author's estate.

"The King" by Alan M. Cvancara. Copyright © 2010 Alan M. Cvancara. Originally appeared in *Short-Short Stories: For Readers Short of Time* by Alan M. Cvancara. Reprinted by permission of the author.

"The Censors" by Luisa Valenzuela. Copyright © Luisa Valenzuela. Reprinted by permission of the author.

"The Memory Priest of the Creech People" by Paul Theroux, published in *Harper's* August 1998 issue. Copyright © 1998 Paul Theroux, used by permission of the Wylie Agency LLC.

"The People Who Owned the Bible" by Will Shetterly. Copyright © Will Shetterly. Originally appeared in *And Other Stories* by Emma Bull and Will Shetterly. Reprinted by permission of the author.

"A Fable" by Robert Fox. Copyright © Robert Fox. Reprinted by permission of the author's estate.

"College Queen" by William Brandon. Copyright © 1947, 1948, 1949, 1950, 1951, 1952, 1953, United Newspapers Magazine Corporation. Originally appeared in *This Week.* Reprinted by permission of the author's estate.

"To Serve Man" by Damon Knight. Original copyright © 1950 Damon Knoght. Originally published in *The Magazine of Fantasy and Science Fiction, winter-spring 1950.* Reprinted by permission of Infinity-Box Press LLC, Portland, OR.

"An Old Man" by Guy de Maupassant, translated by Francis Steegmuller. Originally appeared in *A Lion in the Path* by Francis Steegmuller. Public domain.

"Charles" from "The Lottery" by Shirley Jackson. Copyright © 1948, 1949 Shirley Jackson. Copyright renewed 1976, 1977 by Laurence Hyman, Barry Hyman, Sarah Wester, and Joanne Schnurer. Reprinted by permission of Farrar, Straus and Giroux LLC.

"Mind over Mayhem" by Mack Reynolds. Copyright © 1950, 1978 Wildside Press; first appeared in *New Detective*; reprinted by permission of Wildside Press and the Virginia Kidd Agency Inc.

"The World Where Wishes Worked" by Stephen Goldin, copyright © 1971 Ballantine Books Inc. Reprinted by permission of the author.

"Many Happy Returns" by Justin Case. Copyright © 1966 Davis Publications Inc., for *Ellery Queen's Mystery Magazine.* Reprinted by permission of the Hugh B. Cave estate.

"They're Made out of Meat" by Terry Bisson. Copyright © 1991 Terry Bisson. Reprinted by permission of the author.

# INTRODUCTION

$T$*eaching Information Literacy through Short Stories* examines information literacy themes with eighteen short stories. The book is designed to be interdisciplinary and to be useful in any course or workshop introducing and teaching information literacy skills. Although the use of stories is common in many academic endeavors, scanning the professional literature and information literacy exercises suggests that few, if any, teachers or librarians are using stories to introduce, explain, and expand on the deeper, conceptual, and lifelong goals of information literacy.

There are two basic questions we must ask ourselves. Why should we use stories to understand information literacy? What are the basic motivations of students? Drawing from Roselle's *Transformations II: Understanding American History through Science Fiction*, stories can be used to:

- Stimulate the imaginations of students.
- Increase recognition of the persistent problems that people face.
- Develop the ability to see relationships.
- Facilitate the student's task of understanding.
- Provide bases for analyses of key issues.
- Serve as strong incentives for additional research and study.
- Add immeasurably to the student's enjoyment of social studies. (Roselle, 1974, p. 9)

This list works just as well for teaching information literacy. Adding to and adapting Roselle's list for information literacy instruction, the use of stories enables students and teachers to gain a deeper understanding of:

- The benefits of information literacy.
- The hazards and consequences of information illiteracy.
- The reasons for becoming information literate.
- The desire to build and sustain information literacy skills over a lifetime.

Stories help us to learn what is valuable and to "unlearn" what is not. A good deal of information literacy instruction involves helping students unlearn poor habits of mind. It is easier for a student to embrace a new idea than to kick an old habit. Through the thoughts and actions of story characters, information literacy and illiteracy can be explored. Additionally, stories have four compelling characteristics that make them successful mediums to teach information literacy standards: meaning, memory, fun, and efficiency.

## Stories Provide Meaning

Stories respond to the universal need for meaning. One of the most important tasks in delivering any type of academic instruction is helping students to find meaning somewhere between the assignments and the assessments. It is well known that many students lose the desire to learn for the sake of learning. Many believe the purpose of higher education is to train for a job. To move beyond solely vocational reasons for education, we need to provide students with alternative reasons, rather than methods, for learning in general and for information literacy in particular. Many information literacy exercises emphasize technical skills, such as the introduction to key databases, the principles of online searching, familiarity with different classification systems and information formats, the mechanics of citing resources, and acquainting students with copyright and plagiarism. Although all of these activities are important, they are uninspiring and fail to give meaning and clarity to information literacy. Technical understanding is not enough. An approach that limits itself to instructing students to finding and evaluating information for literature reviews or research papers encourages students to speak and think about information literacy in a utilitarian, linear, and mechanical way. By shuttling between databases or focusing on what buttons to click next in online tutorials, teachers shut out the potential to include philosophical argument and debate about the importance and multiple meanings of information literacy. By promoting the development of individual skills, it decreases the potential to introduce students to the social dimensions of information literacy. Storytelling is a way to provide images of information literacy used for personal, social, and global purposes.

Because meaning does not simply leap from the pages of any story, the teacher must work with students to produce it. As Caine and Caine put it:

> Because the learner is constantly searching for connections on many levels, educators need to *orchestrate the experiences* from which learners extract understanding. They must do more than simply provide information or force the memorization of isolated facts and skills. (1991, p. 5)

Simmons echoes this point:

> A good story helps you influence the interpretation people give to facts. Facts aren't influential until they *mean* something to someone. A story delivers a context so that your facts slide into new slots in your listeners' brains. (2001, p. 51)

Our central point is that we do not use stories to show how to become information literate but why. We use stories to provide students with a variety of reasons about why they should become lifelong learners.

## Stories Aid Memory

Stories are sticky. To put it simply, a good story is easy to remember. Indeed, a good story can last a lifetime. They provide us with a tool to combat the short-term learning formula found in many of today's assessment-dominated classrooms: do the work, take the test, get the grade, forget the work. This sentiment is expressed by Caine and Caine:

Stories and myths help tie content together and aid natural memory. . . . Stories are powerful because they "bind" information and understanding over time. In fact, there is strong reason to believe that the organization of information in story form is a natural brain process. (1991, p. 113)

Like an infectious song, stories wrap themselves around our minds. Rather than simply filling students with discrete and arcane bits of knowledge and skills easily forgotten, stories can be recalled long after the course.

## Stories Make Learning Fun

Stories are fun. As education and entertainment merge, the urge to find interesting and attention-getting tools for learning is an important determinant in pedagogical success. Kurt Cobain, the former lead singer and songwriter of the grunge rock band *Nirvana*, expressed the expectations of today's youth well in the song *Smells like Teen Spirit*, singing, "Here we are now; entertain us!"

Whether we like it or not, many students come to class "having learned that learning is a form of entertainment or, more precisely, that anything worth learning can take the form of entertainment" (Postman, 1985, p. 154). Although we are not advocating "funderstanding" or full-scale "edutainment," we are trying to find a middle ground that is interesting, playful, and substantive. Because many students find stories inherently fun, they offer us a tool to meet several of our goals without resorting to mere amusement.

## Stories Are Time-efficient

One important element of the short story's utility is efficiency. Although many students love stories, they do not enjoy reading. Consequently, the stories selected for this book are short—very short. For students, the short story's brief length means they are more likely to complete the reading. In a society wherein students face increasing demands on their time, efficiently completing assignments is attractive. Because short stories require less time to discover themes than literary alternatives such as the novel, they offer an optimum method for introducing and exploring a large number of information literacy concepts. For instructors, short stories are compatible with a variety of instruction settings, from one-shot sessions to semester-long courses. With the one-shot sessions, it is more realistic to assign a short story to students than a novel. For a semester-long course, a collection of short stories can be assigned. These stories can be read quickly in class or assigned beforehand and discussed in class.

Though the short story differs from the novel in length, there is no definitive minimum or maximum word count. Howe and Howe define the typical short story falling between three and eight thousand words (1982, p. x). In *A Glossary of Literary Terms*, the entry for "short story" includes a description from Edgar Allan Poe, often referred to as the originator of the short story as an established genre. Poe identifies the short story "as a narrative which can be read at one sitting of from half an hour to two hours." This entry in the *Glossary* continues by explaining that the term *short story* "covers a great diversity of prose fiction, all the way from the short short story . . . to such long and complex forms as Herman Melville's *Billy Budd*" (Abrams, 1993, p. 194). It is the subcategory *short short story* that we found most effective and relied on for our selections. This subcategory of short story has various labels, such as micro stories, sudden fiction, flash fiction, and more.

## Framework for Information Literacy for Higher Education

Few if any of the stories selected in this book are explicitly about information literacy. The story authors did not intend on providing imaginative accounts of the need to be information literate. All the stories do, however, illustrate ideas found in the Association of College and Research Libraries (ACRL) *Framework for Information Literacy for Higher Education*. Following the ACRL framework, this book supports the argument that good information literacy instruction is more than teaching students how to find information for their course assignments in an expeditious manner. The *Framework for Information Literacy for Higher Education* encourages the design of assignments that "foster engagement" with higher forms of thinking in information literacy. Stories are a wonderful tool to do that. Stories offer a starting place for more complicated thinking about the purpose of information literacy.

The questions that follow each story here provide a scaffold for conversations about each of the six frames in the *Framework*.

Instructors can use these stories throughout the semester to introduce or reinforce information literacy themes. For those team teaching, these stories can be used to solicit different disciplinary perspectives. For example, a librarian or archivist might use the story "The Liberation of Rome" to introduce general information literacy concepts or the problems experienced by those using libraries or archives to conduct historical research. A historian might then take his or her turn discussing the same story and bring up unique challenges and limitations that historians experience when conducting research. This last point bears underscoring. Information literacy should not be the sole responsibility of a single instructor or discipline. Students benefit from multiple perspectives and methods when making sense of information literacy. Hearing, for example, a librarian, archivist, historian, and archaeologist discuss different disciplinary aspects of the same story better enables students to extend their ideas of the importance of information literacy. Stories offer a vehicle to do this as well as a tool to develop more successful collaborations among librarians and other instructors.

Though this book is not written exclusively for librarians, many librarians may have an interest in it because it pertains to information literacy. We are aware that some academic librarians are likely to argue that the limitations of the typical fifty-minute, one-shot instruction session prevent them from using the stories. Some librarians might also argue that they must respond to what academic faculty request, and this is often introducing students to the library's subscription databases and searching techniques rather than stories containing information literacy themes. Although they would like to use more creative teaching methods such as stories, they can't. Yet while this may be the case for some, it is not the case for all. Some librarians teach semester-long, credit-bearing courses and have time to use the stories throughout the semester. Those using a "flipped" classroom method can assign the stories before class. Others teaching online courses can integrate the stories and related discussions in live chats or blogs. And, as described above, those who are "team teaching" can use the stories in an interdisciplinary fashion. In addition to having students read and discuss the stories, those who are unconstrained by a fifty-minute time limit can require individual or groups of students to write short stories incorporating information literacy themes. Finally, we have found that librarians responding to faculty requests to provide hands-on searching in fifty-minute one-shots can often find some time to supplement this instruction with stories at the beginning or end of the session.

This book is divided into six sections. Each section covers a different frame in ACRL's *Framework for Information Literacy for Higher Education* and includes three stories. Each story is followed by questions to stimulate thought and discussion about different aspects of each frame. Because reading for meaning can sometimes be challenging, one question in each story is dedicated to helping readers think about the meaning of the story as it pertains to an information literacy theme. Like many stories, the lesson is often some variation of "don't do this."

We hope this book will inspire and enable those teaching information literacy to use short stories in their lessons. By reading and reflecting on the stories, students may come to a deeper understanding of information literacy.

## Note

This introduction is a revised form of the article David J. Brier & Vickery Kaye Lebbin, (2004) "Teaching information literacy using the short story," *Reference Services Review*, 32(4), 383–87.

## References

Abrams, M. H. (1993). *A Glossary of Literary Terms*. 6th ed. Fort Worth, TX: Harcourt Brace College Publishers.

Caine, R. N., & Caine, G. (1991). *Making Connections: Teaching and the Human Brain*. Alexandria, VA: Association for Supervision and Curriculum Development.

Howe, I., & Howe, I. (Eds.). (1982). *Short Shorts: An Anthology of the Shortest Stories*. Boston, MA: David R. Godine.

Postman, N. (1985). *Amusing Ourselves to Death: Public Discourse in the Age of Show Business*. New York, NY: Penguin Books.

Roselle, D. (Ed.). (1974). *Transformations II: Understanding American History through Science Fiction*. Greenwich, CT: Fawcett Publications.

Simmons, A. (2001). *The Story Factor: Secrets of Influence from the Art of Storytelling*. Cambridge, MA: Perseus Publishing.

# I

# AUTHORITY IS CONSTRUCTED AND CONTEXTUAL

**A**uthority is an important consideration when confronted with or making an argument. When evaluating an argument, you should think critically about the quality of the reasons and evidence used to support it. Part of this process includes asking questions about the people and organizations making particular claims. The stories in this section explore the idea of authority in different ways.

In T. E. D. Klein's "Renaissance Man," a scientist working in Harvard's physics department is brought from the future to the present in a time machine and then questioned about how things work in a number of unrelated subject areas. The story touches on the nature of expertise and the limits of disciplinary knowledge.

"The Liberation of Rome" by Robin Hemley tells a story about a woman who claims to be a member of a long-thought vanished tribe, the Vandals, and the difficulties of judging the reliability of such a claim. The story invites us to consider how one version of the truth becomes the official, authoritative account of events and how others become marginalized or forgotten.

In James E. Thompson's "The Amphibious Cavalry Gap," an American military adviser provides intelligence on the former Soviet Union's military capabilities and intentions. The story implicitly raises questions about where an information source comes from, its purpose, and the context in which the information is presented. In two short pages, the story demonstrates several blunders in critical thinking and provides food for thought about the trustworthiness of an information source.

The stories in this section illustrate the "Authority Is Constructed and Contextual" frame in textbox 1.1.

Textbox 1.1
**Authority Is Constructed and Contextual**
**Information resources reflect their creators' expertise and credibility and are evaluated based on the information need and the context in which the information will be used. Authority is constructed in that various communities may recognize different types of authority. It is contextual in that the information need may help to determine the level of authority required.**

Experts understand that authority is a type of influence recognized or exerted within a community. Experts view authority with an attitude of informed skepticism and an openness to new perspectives, additional voices, and changes in schools of thought. Experts understand the need to determine the validity of the information created by different authorities and to acknowledge biases that privilege some sources of authority over others, especially in terms of others' worldviews, gender, sexual orientation, and cultural orientations. An understanding of this concept enables novice learners to critically examine all evidence—be it a short blog post or a peer-reviewed conference proceeding—and to ask relevant questions about origins, context, and suitability for the current information need. Thus, novice learners come to respect the expertise that authority represents while remaining skeptical of the systems that have elevated that authority and the information created by it. Experts know how to seek authoritative voices, but also recognize that unlikely voices can be authoritative, depending on need. Novice learners may need to rely on basic indicators of authority, such as type of publication or author credentials, whereas experts recognize schools of thought or discipline-specific paradigms.
**Knowledge Practices**
Learners who are developing their information literate abilities

- define different types of authority, such as subject expertise (e.g., scholarship), societal position (e.g., public office or title), or special experience (e.g., participating in a historic event);
- use research tools and indicators of authority to determine the credibility of sources, understanding the elements that might temper this credibility;
- understand that many disciplines have acknowledged authorities, such as well-known scholars and publications that are widely considered "standard," but that some scholars would challenge the authority of those sources;
- recognize that authoritative content may be packaged formally or informally and may include sources of all media types;
- acknowledge they are developing their own authoritative voices in a particular area and recognize the responsibilities this entails, including seeking accuracy and reliability, respecting intellectual property, and participating in communities of practice;
- understand the increasingly social nature of the information ecosystem where authorities actively connect with one another and sources develop over time.

## Dispositions

Learners who are developing their information literate abilities

- develop and maintain an open mind when encountering varied and sometimes conflicting perspectives;
- motivate themselves to find authoritative sources, recognizing that authority may be conferred or manifested in unexpected ways;
- develop awareness of the importance of assessing content with a skeptical stance and with a self-awareness of their own biases and worldview;
- question traditional notions of granting authority and recognize the value of diverse ideas and worldviews;
- are conscious that maintaining these attitudes and actions requires frequent self-evaluation.

## RENAISSANCE MAN BY T. E. D. KLEIN

Everyone cheered when the little man told them he was a scientist.

Theoretical physicists danced beside their computers; electronics technicians whooped and hollered, abandoning their instrument panels. The huge laboratory rang with the applause of the assembled journalists, and Salganik of the *Herald* was moved to describe the scene as "reminiscent of the jubilation NASA workers demonstrated years ago during the Apollo space shots."

"Thank God!" said Dr. Bazza, an Italian biochemist.

"Thank God he's not a janitor!"

The reporter looked up from his notes. "Pardon me, sir. You were saying. . . ?"

"Thank God we pulled back a man who'll be able to tell us something."

"Was there really that much doubt?" asked Salganik, his pencil poised, prepared to take it all down.

"But of course there was," replied the Italian. "We knew we'd pull back someone from the Harvard Physics Department, because we're here in the building right now. But it could have been just *anyone*. We might have found ourselves questioning a college freshman. . . . Or a scrubwoman. . . . Or even a tourist visiting the lab. We couldn't be sure exactly where our ATV would appear—"

"ATV," said the reporter, feverishly writing in his notebook. "That's 'area of temporal vacuity,' of course?"

"Correct. Rather like those devices you Americans used back in the 1970s, on your interplanetary probes, to collect random samplings of soil. Only this time we've scooped up a living human being, and from our own world. The man is simply—how shall I say it—a random sampling."

"But not *completely* random, I hope. . . ."

"Oh, no, of course not. We knew that our ATV would appear somewhere in the vicinity of this physics lab; we assumed that it would remain a site for advanced research for years to come. But our notion of locality was really quite vague—just a building. And as for time, we simply knew that our visitor"—he gestured toward the little man, who was smiling and shaking his head in wonder—"would come from somewhere three to four hundred years in the future."

Salganik stared across the room at the new celebrity, now surrounded by cameras and lights. He could have gotten a better view, of course, by watching the television screen on the wall nearby—for the scientist's six-hour sojourn in the present was being televised, in its entirety, around the world—but he preferred to watch the little man with his own eyes. *I was there*, he'd be able to tell his grandchildren. *I was right there in the room when we plucked a man out of the future.*

Some idiot journalist had yelled out the traditional "how does it feel? question ("How does it feel to be the first man on the moon?" they used to ask. "How does it feel to win seven gold medals? How does it feel to know that your wife and family have been wiped out by a meteor? How does it feel be elected President?"), and the little man was attempting a reply.

"Well," he was saying, blinking at the lights, "it was all pretty unexpected, this happening to me and all. I mean, I've never won anything in my life, and I never could have imagined that *I*, of all people, would be the one to . . . You know. Be here like this. And I want to say that it's certainly a great *honour* and all, and that I'm certainly as proud as can be to find myself here with you, even if it's only for so short a time . . . Umm. . . ." He bit his lip, blinking at the lights. "I'm happy to say that my era is a really, um *advanced* one—at least *we* think it is, ha ha! 'A Third Renaissance of Learning and Scientific Achievement,' that's the motto of the World's Fair over in Addis Ababa. . . . A renaissance rivalling the one in the early 2200—but of course you wouldn't know about that, would you? Hmmm . . . I'm not really a very good speaker, you see, but, um . . . I sure hope I'll be able to provide you knowledge that will maybe interest you and, um, *help* a bit, maybe?"

He smiled bashfully.

"It's remarkable!" muttered Dr. Bazza. "You'd think the language might have changed over the centuries, but this man speaks English better than I do! Perhaps it was cinema that stabilized the language. . . ."

"And a good thing too," whispered Salganik. "If this project turned out to be a fiasco—if you guys had materialized a three-year-old baby, or some moron with nothing to say—the government would pull its money out so fast you'd get dizzy."

He remembered how hard NASA had tried to persuade Congress that the lunar explorers were carrying back valuable scientific information—that half a dozen bags of moon rubble were worth all those billions of dollars. In the end Congress had deemed the missions "impractical" and had discontinued them. The men in this lab had been under the same kind of pressure. . . .

But it looked as if they'd made a lucky catch.

"Oh, yes," the man was saying, "I've been a professor of plasmic biophysics for almost . . . Let me see . . . nearly twenty-eight years."

"Could you tell us what that means?" shouted one of the reporters who had crowded his way toward the front.

Immediately a storm of abuse broke over his head: *Hush! Please! Expel this man! Ssshh! We'll get to that later! Quiet!*

Reporters were supposed to remain silent, leaving all questions to a panel of scientists who, it was hoped, could make better use of the limited time. That other reporter's questions had wasted enough time already. . . .

"Professor," asked Dr. Sklar, the Nobel Prize–winning pathologist, "let's start with the most vital issues first." He spoke solemnly, aware that the world was listening to every word. "I shall not even pause to ask your name—"

"Modesto 14X Goodyear," interrupted the little man.

"—or to find out anything about yourself. Those of us gathered here are interested in solving some of our most pressing problems. To begin with—"

He paused portentously, allowing the drama to grow.

"—have men in your time found *a cure for cancer?*"

The visitor smiled. "Oh my *gosh* yes," he replied. "We hardly even *talk* about cancer any more. I mean, the only ones who come down with it these days are men in deep space, and . . ."

Sklar cut him off. "Can you explain to us how it is cured?" There was urgency in his voice.

"Whew!" said the little man, puffing out his cheeks and glancing toward the ceiling. "Hmmm, let's see. That *is* a toughie, I'm afraid." He looked blank for several seconds. "You see, I've never had cancer myself, and few people I know have . . . But if we got it, we'd ring for a physician, and he'd come and, um . . ."

"What would he do?"

"Well, he'd give us this drug, and then we'd just . . . sleep it off, I guess you'd say."

"This drug?" demanded Sklar.

"Yes, well, I'm afraid I only know the brand name—Gro-Go-Way, it's called. But I suppose that's not much help to you. . . ."

Dr. Sklar looked disappointed.

"You see, that's not really my field," explained the visitor, with an embarrassed shrug.

"A moment ago you spoke of 'ringing for a physician,'" said another panelist. (Dr. Sklar was now busy writing down new questions.) "I'm a communications engineer and I wonder if you might tell us something about communications in your day."

"Delighted."

"For example, what exactly happens when you ring for the doctor?"

"Why, he comes immediately. Or at least he's *supposed* to. But I don't mind telling you, quite often you get *rude* and *shoddy* treatment, he'll tell you he's too *busy* right now and—"

"Please, sir! How does the thing work? Do you have instruments like this? The engineer pointed toward a nearby table. "Telephones?"

"Oh, telephones! Yes, sure we have them, only they don't look like that. My, oh my, what an antique *that* would make. . . . No, ours fit behind your ear." He reached back behind his own. "Oh dear, I've left mine off today, otherwise I'd show you . . . But anyway, it's different when we ring for a physician. Then we press a red button in the bathroom, right by the bed, and we describe our—But you look confused."

"No, no, go on."

"We just say, in effect, 'I feel sick, send somebody over.'"

"And who's on the other end?"

"Well . . . *people*. And they hear me and send help." He paused, looking a little doubtful. "Of course, it takes a few minutes."

"And how does all this work? Explain the mechanism."

"Gee," said the scientist from the future, "I'm sure I don't know. I never really bothered to find out. I mean, it's always been there on the wall, and I just . . . I feel guilty as hell, but I mean, it's just not my field. I deal almost exclusively with a type of chromosomatic plant nodule, they're called Phillips' bodies, and . . . Well, let me say *this* about communications: those people on the other end of the line are by no means the most efficient in the world, believe me, the service is *atrocious* these days and they're forever going out on strike for one reason or another, so . . ."

"Weapons!" spoke up a general. "What are the most sophisticated weapons in your military's arsenal?"

"Well, we have no military *per se*, but . . . Oh, yes, we *do* have some horrible weapons at our disposal, oh *my* yes. There's one called a VRV—I'm not sure what the letters stand for—that can leave a four-teen-meter deep crater where a city used to be, and the neighbouring towns won't even be touched. One was actually used—on San Juan, Puerto Rico."

"How does it work?"

"Hmmm . . . You got me. I'm afraid I'm stumped." He paused, looking downcast—and then brightened. "You know, you want to talk to a nuclear engineer about that. Your best bet would be a fellow named Julio 6X Franklin, an old friend . . . Though of course that's impossible right now, isn't it? Hmmm . . . I *think* I read somewhere that it uses the same principle as the moon pulling on the tides—moon on the tides, does that sound right?—but I'm really not the man to see."

Salganik leaned toward his companion. "I hate to say it," he whispered, "but this guy doesn't know anything about anything. What gives?"

But Dr. Bazza only shook his head. He looked as if he were about to cry.

The little man was attempting to explain the construction of the anti-gravity belt his son wore when walking on lakes. "It broke down once and we had to have the repairman over. He . . . Let me see, he told me it had a battery, yes, and a triangular chunk of this spongy substance . . . Levia, I think it's called, but I don't know exactly what it's made of. Zinc, maybe?

The scientists had stopped taking notes long ago.

Dr. Bazza turned to Salganik. "Listen," he pleaded, his voice edged with desperation, "how much do you think *you'd* know if you went back into the Dark Ages? Could *you* tell them how to build an airplane? Or perform an appendectomy? Or make nylon? What good would *you* be?"

Salganik shrugged. "I guess . . ." he ventured. "I guess that, even during the Renaissance, there weren't many Renaissance Men."

The cameras and tape-recorders continued to whir.

"I recall looking over the repairman's shoulder when he replaced the battery," the little man was saying, "and there was this little bundle of wires . . ."

## Questions for Students to Discuss

1. Why did everyone cheer when they learned a scientist from the future was pulled back in time?
2. Why did the author choose to have the scientist from Harvard University?
3. When describing Modesto 14X Goodyear, a professor of plasmic biophysics, at the end of the story, Salganik says, "This guy doesn't know anything about anything." To what degree do you or don't you agree with Salganik's opinion? Why?
4. Klein's story preconceives what it means to be an authority. What is that conception?
5. If you could speak with one person from the future to answer the questions posed in this story, whom would you choose? Justify your answer.
6. What is the moral of this story regarding authority?

## THE LIBERATION OF ROME BY ROBIN HEMLEY

A young woman named Amy Buleric sat in my office looking down at her feet. I figured someone had died, or maybe she was having emotional problems, or was sick. I bolstered myself for whatever horror or misfortune she might throw my way. A colleague of mine forces students to bring in obituaries when they claim a relative has died, but I think that's pathetic. I'd rather believe a student and risk being a fool than become power-crazed. So I was bolstering myself because I was afraid to hear what Amy Buleric was going to tell me about the reason for her absence for the last three weeks.

One time a student sent me a note, "Dr. Radlisch, I'm sorry I can't finish the paper on Hannibal for you." The next day I learned the boy had killed himself—not because of my paper, of course. He had problems I only found out about later. He must have sent me that note out of a pitiful sense of duty. Still, his words haunt me even today.

This young woman was fidgety, not looking at me, and so I sat there patiently, waiting for her to find the courage to tell me whatever it was that bothered her.

"Dr. Radlisch," she said finally, her voice almost a whisper.

"Take your time, Amy," I said, just as softly.

She looked past me to one of my bookshelves. "Why do you have that sign in your office?"

I sat up and turned around so quickly that a muscle popped in my neck. The sign was hand-lettered, done by a friend of my daughter, Claudia, who specializes in calligraphy for weddings. It reads, "If Rome be weak, where shall strength be found?"

"It's a quote from the poet Lucan," I said.

"Yes, I know," she said, a bangled arm sweeping aside her hair. She looked at me with what seemed suddenly like defiance and contempt. "But why is it here? It's . . . like . . . propaganda."

"I'm not sure I understand what you're saying, Amy," I said. I sat back in my chair. My thoughts, my voice became formal. "I thought we were here to discuss your absences, any problems you've been having."

I saw she was about to cry, so I stopped. "I mean," I said, softening my voice, "it's hard to find a solution unless I know what's wrong. Still, I'm glad you stopped in here to talk. I hate it when students simply disappear without a word."

It was too late. She started to cry, and I could see this was the last thing she wanted to do, that she was terribly embarrassed. The tears ran down her face and she didn't make any move to wipe them away.

"I wanted to disappear," she said, "but I couldn't. I had to confront you. That sign is my problem. Part of it anyway."

"Confront me?" I said. I scooted my chair back an inch or two.

"You've probably never had someone like me in one of your classes, and so there was no one to challenge your ideas."

"Ms. Buleric," I said. "I teach Roman history. I don't know what you're talking about. I have no ideas to be challenged. I voice the ideas of the ancients with my tongue, their accounts. I'm not sure where this is all leading, but I thought we were here to talk about your absences."

"I am here to talk about your lies," she said.

I stood up. Amy Buleric didn't rise from her chair and leave as I expected she would. Here I'd thought she needed my sympathy, my help, and she'd only come to accuse me of telling lies.

I sat on the edge of my desk and folded my arms. "How old are you, Amy? Nineteen. Twenty?"

"Twenty," she said.

"Why are you here?" I asked.

"Someone needs to stop you from telling lies."

I waved my hand at her. "Not that. I mean, why are you in college?" I smiled to show I wasn't her enemy. "Do you feel that you know everything already? Or do you think that college might just possibly, just on an outside chance, teach you something—something that might even challenge some of your old notions or the notions of your parents?"

"What about you, Dr. Radlisch?" she said, sitting up straight in her chair. "Do you know everything already? What about your old notions? Can they be challenged?"

"People say I'm open-minded," I said, glancing at my watch.

"I'm here to better my people," she said, looking around the office as though her people had gathered around her.

"Your people? Are you a Mormon?"

"No."

"You're not . . . I mean, you don't look . . ."

"I'm a Vandal, Dr. Radlisch."

I put my chin in my hand. "A Vandal," was all I could manage to say.

"Part Vandal," she said. "Over half."

"You deface property?" I said.

"Another lie," she said. "Another stinking Roman lie." She spat on my carpet.

"You spat on my carpet," I told her and pointed to it.

"I'm a Vandal, Dr. Radlisch," she said. "If you only knew the truth about us."

"Amy," I said calmly. "I'm not doubting you, of course. But what you're telling me is that you're a Vandal. V-A-N-D-A-L. Vandal. Like the tribe? The one that disappeared from history in the sixth century A.D. when Belisarius defeated them and sold them into slavery?"

"Pig" she said. "Dog. Roman dung. Belisarius." And she spat again.

"Please stop spitting on my carpet," I asked her.

She nodded and folded her arms primly in her lap.

"And you're here in my office to set the record straight," I said.

"There isn't any record, Dr. Radlisch," she said. "That's the point. The Vandal tradition is entirely oral. We don't trust the written word. That was the way of the Romans. 'Lies are the province of Romans and writers.' That's an old Vandal proverb. The only record you have is the record of the Romans. They tell you that we were a war-like people who invaded Gaul at the beginning of the fifth century. But that was only because the Huns attacked us first. They drove us out of the Baltic. And we didn't attack the Gauls. We were just defending ourselves! Then the Franks defeated us in 409 and we fled into Spain. We were only there twenty years when a lying Roman governor invited us into North Africa to establish an independent homeland on the ashes of Carthage. We should have known better than to set up camp in Carthage. The only reason we captured Rome was to stop their oppression of us and other peoples who they had colonized or destroyed. We didn't sack Rome. We liberated it."

She knew her history. Or at least a version, one that I had never heard before.

"And now you're coming forward."

"We've always been here," she said. "You've never noticed."

I wanted to believe her, but I was having a little difficulty. "So for the last fourteen hundred years . . ."

"That's right," she said. "Oh, we've intermarried some, but we've kept our traditions alive." She started to wail. Her eyes were closed and her mouth was stretched in an unnatural grimace. After a minute of this, she stopped, opened her eyes, and wiped her brow.

"Birth song," she announced.

"It's very different," I said. "Haunting."

She seemed pleased that I'd said this. She bowed her head. "For over a millennium our voices have been silenced. No one wanted to hear the Vandal songs. No one cared, though I suppose we were lucky. In some ways, we prefer the world's indifference to its attention. As soon as you're recognized, you're hunted and destroyed. So we waited. And now we're back."

My shoulders tensed and I rubbed my neck where the muscle had popped.

"Thank you for coming forward," I told her. "I know how hard it must be for you. I'm sure there are many things you could teach me."

She smiled at me again and all the anger seemed to be gone. "About the paper that's due?" she said.

"What?"

"Lies are the province of Romans and writers."

At first I didn't get it, but then I saw what she was telling me. "Oh, right," I said. "I guess you can't write it, can you?"

"No, I'm sorry," she said.


## Questions for Students to Discuss

1. Why do you believe that Dr. Radlisch privileged the Roman version of history over the Vandal version of history? Why do or don't you think this was justified?

2. If you were Dr. Radlisch in this story, what questions would you have asked Amy to determine her expertise and credibility?

3. In comparison to Dr. Radlisch, what does and doesn't make Amy an authority? Why might some see Dr. Radlisch as an expert but not Amy? Justify and critique the argument that Dr. Radlisch is an expert on Roman history but Amy is not.

4. Is Dr. Radlisch aware of his biases regarding Roman history? When confronted with Amy's alternative Vandal history, to what degree does he question and evaluate his biases?

5. After Amy tells Dr. Radlisch the Vandal version of history, to what extent does he question the standard view of Roman histo-

ry? What sources and strategies could Dr. Radlisch use to examine the accuracy of the standard view of Roman history?

6. What lesson or lessons about authority can be learned from this story?

## *THE AMPHIBIOUS CAVALRY GAP* BY J. J. TREMBLY AS TOLD TO JAMES E. THOMPSON

J. J. Trembly (Special Adviser, Naval Research and Development Commission on New Weapons Systems) as told to James E. Thompson

Military intelligence estimates of the enemy's strength and plans require two ingredients. One is logic. The other . . .

Intelligence reports coming out of Soviet Central Asia and Siberia indicate that the Soviets have undertaken an extensive horse-breeding program.[1] The number of horses in the USSR increased fifteen percent[2] or forty-two percent[3] in the period 1968–81. These figures indicate that the Soviet planners have assigned horse-breeding a high priority.

The question now arises: What place does this crash program occupy in Soviet strategic thinking? Here we can only speculate; but, in the light of the Soviet Union's known expansionist aims, it behooves us to consider the possibility that they intend to use those horses against us.

Horses have not been used extensively in warfare since the outbreak of World War Two, when the Polish cavalry proved highly ineffective against German armor.[4] This has led to the consensus of military thought—that is, of Western military thought—that cavalry is obsolete. But can we afford to call cavalry "obsolete" when the enemy has not? The Soviet rulers are not talking about cavalry being "obsolete"; instead, as we have seen, they are breeding more horses.

Someone may object that Soviet cavalry cannot pose a threat to the United States, because the two nations have no common land boundary, but are separated by water; and it has been found that cavalry is effective only on land.[5] Cavalry could, however, be used against the United States by the USSR (or vice versa) if the horses and their riders were transported to the scene of combat by sea or air. If the horses are transported by air, this gives no obvious advantage to one side or the other, as all points on the Earth's surface are equally accessible by air; but if we think in terms of the horses being transported by sea, an ominous conclusion emerges. Let us list the most important cities in the two nations. In our case, this will consist of our national capital plus the four most populous cities; in theirs, of the five most populous, as their capital (Moscow) is also the most populous city:[6]

| USSR | USA |
| --- | --- |
| Moscow | Washington |
| Leningrad | New York |
| Kiev | Chicago |
| Tashkent | Los Angeles |
| Kharkov | Philadelphia |

When we look at the location of these cities on the map, we find that only one of the key Soviet cities—Leningrad—is located on the sea, while four of the five key American cities are located on the seacoast or very near it—New York, Philadelphia, Washington and Los Angeles. (And even Chicago might be accessible by sea, via the St. Lawrence seaway.) Therefore, we are at least *four times* as vulnerable to amphibious attack as the USSR. When one considers that they also have more horses than we do, the seriousness of the amphibious cavalry gap becomes apparent.

If the horses are to be transported by sea, it must be either by surface ship or by submarine. We can, I think, rule out the use of surface ships, for submarines have the advantage of concealability; if the horses were transported on the decks of surface ships they could be detected by our sky-spies. So if the Soviets are planning a sneak amphibious cavalry attack on the US, they will almost certainly use submarines, and will be building a larger submarine fleet. This, we find, is precisely what they *are* doing. The Soviet Union now has 401 submarines to only 152 for the United States.[7]

Is there any hope of overcoming the disparity between our military capacity and that of the Soviets caused by our greater vulnerability? In my opinion, there is such a hope; but it can only be achieved by the creation of a greater total striking force proportionate to the enemy's greater invulnerability, that is, four times as many horses, four times as many trained cavalrymen, and four times as many cavalry transport submarines. In the field of submarines alone, this means that, as the Soviets have 401 usable submarines, we need 1,604. Given that our present submarine strength is only 152, we need 1,452 more submarines, to be fitted for cavalry transport, for an adequate defense.

It is urgently necessary that we begin at once to close this gap. The Defense Department should immediately make known the seriousness of the threat, and demand that Congress vote the necessary funds.

Some persons have suggested that a weapons system of the type described poses no real threat; but an experienced submarine commander has assured the author that a cavalry-carrying submarine would be, in his words, "a real *stinker*."

## Notes

1. See DoD Report #BX818RL, "Livestock populations in Soviet Virgin Lands," Washington, DC, 1971.
2. Estimate by CIA.
3. Estimate by US Army Intelligence.
4. Gen. Heinz Guderian, *Panzer Leader*, trans. C. Fitzgibbon. New York: Dutton & Co., 1952, pp. 65–84.
5. See, for example, Exodus 14:26–30.
6. According to population statistics from the 1972 World Almanac.
7. *Jane's Fighting Ships*, 1971–72 ed.

## Questions for Students to Discuss

1. When thinking about the trustworthiness of a source, we need to contextualize it. In "The Amphibious Cavalry Gap," who is J. J. Trembly? What are J. J. Trembly's credentials? Who did J. J. Trembly make this intelligence report for? How might this intelligence report be used? Based on this context, do you agree or disagree that the level of credibility and quality of this source is adequate for the intended purpose? Why do or don't you need a more authoritative source? Justify your answer.
2. The story provides a fictional account of military intelligence gathered for a country that no longer exists (the Union of Soviet Socialist Republics). What if you were a U.S. Senator and had to vote on whether or not to spend billions of dollars to develop a new weapons system to mitigate a security threat from a contemporary country. What types of sources would you trust? For example, why would or wouldn't you trust a blog on the issue authored by an adversary, a Facebook post by a journalist from a

country not involved in the conflict, a tweet by an international nonprofit organization?

3. How would you go about determining where J. J. Trembly obtained the information for his report on the Soviet cavalry? Why would or wouldn't it matter to you if Trembly actually observed the horse-breeding program in the USSR?

4. If you found several scholarly articles by different university professors providing analysis on the rise of the number of horses in the USSR but with very different conclusions in each article, how would you determine which authority is more credible?

5. What are the different ways you can become a trusted expert on horse-breeding programs in different parts of the world? What are the different ways you can become an intelligence expert on defense-related subjects? Why do or don't you believe that some ways of becoming an intelligence expert are better than others? Why do or don't you believe that the way you become an expert shapes the degree to which you can be trusted?

6. Summarize the meaning of the story as it pertains to authority.

# 2

# INFORMATION CREATION AS A PROCESS

You can often choose from a variety of information sources in different formats for your research and assignments. However, you should be aware that each of these sources and formats goes through a different set of actions and steps before the information is published. The "Information Creation As a Process" frame encourages you to think about this process and what it means for your research. The stories in this section help you to examine this frame from a variety of different angles and perspectives.

In "Megaphone" by Rick Cook, an alien delivers an environmental message to a U.S. senator rather than a lobbyist. Cook invites us to consider the extent to which the format the information is contained in matters as much or more than the content of the information.

Nelson Bond's story "The Voice from the Curious Cube" calls into question who is creating information and for what reason and audience. The curious cube is the name given by beings in the future to a mysterious marble slab created by an unseen alien race. Like Cook, Bond draws attention to the importance of format.

In "The King" by Alan M. Cvancara, a professor and graduate student come to different conclusions about the meaning of a fossil. Cvancara's story introduces us to power differences in the research process.

The stories in this section invite us to explore the "Information Creation As a Process" frame in textbox 2.1.

Textbox 2.1

**Information Creation As a Process**

**Information in any format is produced to convey a message and is shared via a selected delivery method. The iterative processes of researching, creating, revising, and disseminating information vary, and the resulting product reflects these differences.**

The information creation process could result in a range of information formats and modes of delivery, so experts look beyond format when selecting resources to use. The unique capabilities and constraints of each creation process as well as the specific information need determine how the product is used. Experts recognize that information creations are valued differently in different contexts, such as academia or the workplace. Elements that affect or reflect on the creation, such as a pre- or post-publication editing or reviewing process, may be indicators of quality. The dynamic nature of information creation and dissemination requires ongoing attention to understand evolving creation processes. Recognizing the nature of information creation, experts look to the underlying processes of creation as well as the final product to critically evaluate the usefulness of the information. Novice learners begin to recognize the significance of the creation process, leading them to increasingly sophisticated choices when matching information products with their information needs.

**Knowledge Practices**

Learners who are developing their information literate abilities

- articulate the capabilities and constraints of information developed through various creation processes;
- assess the fit between an information product's creation process and a particular information need;
- articulate the traditional and emerging processes of information creation and dissemination in a particular discipline;
- recognize that information may be perceived differently based on the format in which it is packaged;
- recognize the implications of information formats that contain static or dynamic information;

- monitor the value that is placed upon different types of information products in varying contexts;
- transfer knowledge of capabilities and constraints to new types of information products;
- develop, in their own creation processes, an understanding that their choices impact the purposes for which the information product will be used and the message it conveys.

## Dispositions

Learners who are developing their information literate abilities

- are inclined to seek out characteristics of information products that indicate the underlying creation process;
- value the process of matching an information need with an appropriate product;
- accept that the creation of information may begin initially through communicating in a range of formats or modes;
- accept the ambiguity surrounding the potential value of information creation expressed in emerging formats or modes;
- resist the tendency to equate format with the underlying creation process;
- understand that different methods of information dissemination with different purposes are available for their use.

## MEGAPHONE BY RICK COOK

*The key,* Senator Steven Cherney told himself, *is to talk a language they'll understand.*

The Virginia dawn was glorious, the late spring air alive with birdsong and the woods were green and lovely. But Cherney's mind was on politics, as usual.

He scuffed the dead leaves thoughtfully with his foot and considered his options carefully. The votes were there to bring the dams and waterways bill out of committee, but there was going to be a messy floor fight unless he could head it off.

Too expensive, they complained. Full of pork, they said. Well, maybe there was something there for a lot of people, but that didn't make it less important to his state's farmers—and those farmers were damned important to him. They'd pulled him through a tough election and now it was his turn.

He had come here, to a friend's farm, as he so often did to get away from the bustle and pressures of the capital. "My own private Camp David," he sometimes called it when he was feeling presidential. He would tramp the woods at dawn and sleep in the upstairs bedroom of a farmhouse which had been old when Union and Confederate armies clashed in its sight. On Monday he would return to the city refreshed, restored and with his plans laid.

*As for the expense, we'll just have to find the money,* he thought. We'll slice someplace to make up for it, something that doesn't have a real constituency. Research? NASA? The bill would go easier if he had a victim lined up beforehand.

Cherney was so absorbed he barely heard the leaves rustle behind him. He remembered the odor of musk and violets and struggling for breath and consciousness. Then nothing.

He awoke on a bench, lying under a sheet. He sat up suddenly and clutched the edge of the bench as the world reeled. He closed his eyes and breathed deeply several times to steady himself and when he opened them he saw he was not alone.

He was, however, the only person in the room.

The creature behind the desk was small, a little over five feet he guessed, humanoid, and frail. Not frail, the senator corrected himself, delicate. Like fine porcelain. What skin he could see was golden brown and hairless. The head was much wider at the top than the bottom so it seemed to balance precariously on the thin neck. But it was the eyes that grabbed his attention. They were huge, dark, and so luminous a man could lose himself forever in them.

*My God!* he thought. *Oh my God!* His heart hammered and he closed his eyes once more against a new wave of dizziness. When he opened them the creature was still there, unmoving, unblinking. He licked his lips and tasted metal, a taste he hadn't known since Vietnam.

*Say something dammit!* This is a historic event, "Ahhh . . . umm." Not exactly famous words or even his usual standard of eloquence, but Senator Steven Cherney was happy to find his mouth worked at all.

The creature raised a thin, inhumanly long arm and Cherney saw that it ended in a knot of worm-like tentacles. The tentacles moved over the surface of a small gray box on the desk and the box spoke.

"Why have you decided not to explore space?" The creature asked, softly, gently and with all the sadness in the world.

"Huh? I mean, I beg your pardon?" Cherney had expected almost anything but that.

"Why have you turned away from space?"

"Forgive us," the box said as the creature stroked it. "But we have to know. There are so very few intelligent races which jump the gap." The tendrils hesitated on the surface and then the voice went on. "And we are lonely, you see."

"But we have an active space program," Cherney protested. "We've been to the Moon, we've sent probes to the outer planets. We've even built a Space Shuttle."

"You use the form of speech for past events." The tone did not change. The voice was as soft and gentle and—regretful?—as ever. "You have done these things and now you do them no more. We wish to understand why." The creature added apologetically, "It is important to us."

"There's the space station . . ." Cherney began and then stopped. He knew all too well what had happened to the space station. How it had been turned from a jumping-off point for planetary exploration into a research base and then whittled down and stretched out repeatedly. He had done some of the whittling himself.

The creature said nothing, only looked at him.

*Hell,* thought Cherney. *How in God's name do you answer a question like that? How do you explain to something from beyond the sky about budget deficits and social needs and priorities in a time of limited resources?* Never mind the really deciding things like deals and quiet understandings. For the first time in a long time, Senator Steven Cherney felt small and inadequate.

"Other things are more important right now," he said finally. "We have problems we must meet first."

"Yet those problems grow constantly worse," the voice said gently, inexorably. "Each year it gets harder for you to devote the resources to exploration. Soon it becomes impossible." The creature gestured. "We have seen it before."

*Fermi paradox,* Cherney thought dully. That's what they call it. Why don't we find signs of intelligent life in the universe? Is that the answer? They all just quit? He had a vision of an alien Budget Committee solemnly holding hearings on its space program. He could even picture old Senator Cronkite with scaly green skin and tentacles waving dramatically as he thundered against the waste of it all.

"Well look," Cherney said. "If it's that important to you why don't you help us? You could show us how to do it."

"That has been tried," the creature said. "It has turned out—badly."

Remembering the plight of his state's Indians Cherney was silent again.

"You said there were other races," he said at last. "How many?"

"Intelligent races? Many. Those that have made the leap to space? Just ourselves." The tentacles paused and then caressed the box again. "Just ourselves."

"What about the others?"

"Most of them do not survive," the voice said sadly.

Cherney's breath caught in his throat. "What happens to them?"

The creature made an odd "palm"-up gesture. "Many things," the box said. "A planet's resources are finite. Eventually a species finds limits to its growth. Some of them battle to extinction, some lay down and die quietly. A very few survive by regression and stagnation."

Cherney went cold. Two years before he had toured refugee camps in Ethiopia on a fact-finding mission on world hunger. The walking skeletons and the children with pipestem legs, enormous dark eyes and swollen bellies would be with him always. Sometimes he had nightmares about those emaciated, dying children and their parents walking the streets of his city.

He licked his lips. "No other choice?" he asked.

The alien inclined its head and stroked the box, "We have found none. In all our searching."

"Oh my God," he breathed.

"As you will," the alien stroked the box again, "Only tell us—why?"

"Because we're fools," Senator Steven Cherney snapped. "We're blind, stupid fools who will dig our own graves if we're given half a chance." The alien reached for its box and he held up a hand to interrupt it.

"But we're something else too," he said, lapsing into the style he'd learned as a kid sergeant leading a squad in the Delta. "We're fighters and we don't quit. Stopped? No, we've just paused. And I'll tell you another thing. We're about through pausing. We would have gone on anyway because it's always been our way to push over the next hill. But that pause will end one holy hell of a lot quicker when I get back to Washington.

"No, whoever you are. You're not going to be alone much longer. We're coming out to you and we're coming fast. By God, we will not lay down and die!"

Senator Steven Cherney realized his cheeks were wet and that he really didn't give a damn. It felt good to go beyond all the shitty compromises and arcane maneuverings that had brought him where he was; to have a clear simple goal and to know it was worth fighting for with every ounce of breath in his body. Besides everything else, it felt good.

The alien inclined its head. "It is not an easy thing to do."

He grinned mirthlessly. "We've got a saying. The difficult we do immediately. The impossible takes a little longer. Keep looking up, fella, because you're going to have something to see damn quick."

The alien fingers caressed the box. "That is your answer?"

Steven Cherney, once a sergeant in Company K, 1st Battalion First Air Cavalry and now the junior senator from his state squared his shoulders and stared deep into the dark eyes before him. "Damn straight."

"Then you have told us what we wish to know," the box said, less regretfully. "Thank you." The creature lifted its hand from the box and gestured. Cherney smelled musk and violets and dizziness washed over him again.

The alien's final words seemed to come from the bottom of a deep, distant well. "And good luck."

He awoke under a tree on the hill overlooking the farmhouse. The sky had turned slate gray and thunder muttered through it. He raised his head, felt the familiar dizziness and then settled back to rest, thinking.

His aides wouldn't appreciate being rousted for an evening staff meeting, but he had to get rolling. It was already late in the session to schedule new hearings, not to mention the deals that would have to be cut to make things happen. As he lay there his politician's brain went into high gear, weighing alternative approaches, considering potential allies and maneuvers.

One thing he was not going to do was tell anyone what had happened. The last thing he needed was to be front-page news in every supermarket tabloid in the country. No, he'd come up with some reasonable, plausible explanation for his new policy—and then he would push like hell to get the space program rolling.

"We're going to do it," he said to the leaden sky. "By God, we'll make that jump. Just see if we don't." It began to sprinkle lightly as Senator Steven Cherney got slowly to his feet and started on the path back.

"It's all in the presentation," said the golden-skinned alien, tugging roughly at her antennae. They came away, and with them large chunks of latex makeup. A few more tugs and the woman underneath was revealed. She was tiny with dark hair and eyes almost as dark as the costume's—even if they weren't as luminous.

"I still say this is a crazy idea," said the tall, slender man who was carefully cleaning latex "skin" and makeup off the tentacled "hands" before packing the delicate mechanisms in their storage case.

"Then why did you turn down a job with Spielberg to fly clear across the country to help us with it?"

He grinned, "Hell, Sis, you know I could never resist a challenge. And you've got to admit, that's some makeup job."

"I'll say," the woman agreed. "I think my skin ages ten years every time I put it on."

"Well, there's just one more to go," said the second man, as he repacked the oxygen mask. "I'll be glad when this is over. Aside from details like legality, that knockout gas is dangerous."

"What is that stuff anyway?" the other man asked.

The man with the oxygen mask grinned, "Ethyl chloride with some scent added. It's fast, but it's tricky as hell and I'd hate to OD someone on it."

"It's in a good cause," the small woman said as she began to pull the fake skin off her arms. "One more senator and our list will be complete."

"I'm still surprised no one has said anything," said the anesthesiologist.

The other man smiled, "That was the one thing we were sure wouldn't happen. These men are realists. That means that to them unreal things like their reputations are the most important things in the world. They won't talk."

"Do you really think this will do any good?" the doctor asked.

The woman frowned, "You mean can we change the course of history? No. But we can attract attention. So far we've pulled this gag on five key people: Two Congressmen, a NASA official, a White House staffer and now a senator. The ones who have been major stumbling blocks. With them either convinced or neutralized, maybe we can get some momentum into space again."

"Lobbying would be a whole lot more legal," her brother said neutrally.

The woman's eyes sparkled. "Yeah, but lobbying's not nearly as much fun."

"Besides which it doesn't work," the doctor said practically. "We've tried. It isn't that people like Cherney disagree with us, they're just more concerned with other things. We can't speak loudly enough to be heard in their scheme of things. So we present them with someone or something they will listen to."

"And we're telling them the truth," the woman said, ripping off another chunk of her face in an angry gesture and wincing as the latex pulled her skin raw. "You've seen the computer simulations. You know where they lead."

"Still, it seems immoral to me," her brother said.

She smiled sweetly, luminously. "So was the bill of goods Columbus sold Isabella." Then she reached for the jar of cold cream. "Now come on, let's get ready for the next one."

## Questions for Students to Discuss

1. When reflecting on the effectiveness of her communication with Senator Cherney, the woman pretending to be an alien said, "It's all in the presentation." In other words, the format and delivery method are the most important factors influencing the effectiveness of the message. But why? What makes this so? Why is or isn't the accurateness of the content of the information conveyed more important than the presentation? What implication does this have in real life in, say, political messages or advertising?

2. If the senator received the message from the alien, in, say, a blog or a tweet, why do or don't you think this format and delivery method would be as effective as a personal delivery?

3. To what extent did the senator consider the process behind the alien's information and message? In other words, to what degree did the senator ask about the actions or steps that the alien took to conclude that his species was the only intelligent race that made "the leap to space" and that humans must do so as well to ensure their long-term survival?

4. Why did the people behind the hoax choose to use an alien rather than a lobbyist to deliver their message to Senator Cherney?

5. What effects might photographs of the alien have had on other members of Congress if Senator Cherney shared his private encounter with an alien? Why do or don't you think photographs would change their perception of his credibility? What is it about a photograph versus, say, another format such as text or an audio recording that might change the way they think about his story?

6. Using at least one aspect of the "Information Creation As a Process" frame, what is the moral of the story?

## THE VOICE FROM THE CURIOUS CUBE BY NELSON BOND

All Xuthil seethed with excitement. The broad highways, the swirling ramps that led to the public forum were thronged with the jostling bodies of a hundred thousand inhabitants, while in the living quarters of the capital city millions unable to witness the spectacle first-hand waited anxiously by their *menavisors* for news.

The curious cube had opened. The gigantic slab of marble, its sheer, glistening walls towering hundreds of feet above the head of the tallest Xuthilian, its great square base more than a hundred home-widths on each side, but a few hours ago had opened—one smoothly oiled block sliding backward to reveal a yawning pit of blackness in its depths.

Already a band of daring explorers, heavily armed, had penetrated the depths of the curious cube. Soon they would return to make a public report, and it was this which all Xuthil breathlessly awaited.

None living knew the purpose—or dared guess the fearful age—of the curious cube. The earliest archives in Xuthilian libraries noted its existence, presupposing divine origin or construction. For certainly even the accomplished hands of earth's dominate race could not have built so gigantic a structure. It was the work of Titans, or a god.

So, with *menavisors* dialed to the forum for the first mental images to be broadcast therefrom by members of the exploration party, Xuthil hummed with nervous activity.

Abruptly a pale green luminescence flooded the reflector screens of the *menavisors*, and a thrill coursed through the viewers. The exploration party had returned. Tul, chief of all Xuthilian scientists, was stepping upon the circular dais, his broad, intelligent forehead furrowed with thought. His band of followers trailed after him. They too walked leadenly.

Tul stepped before the image-projecting unit. As he did so, a wavering scene began to impress itself into the minds of his watchers—a picture that grew more clear and distinct as the mental contact strengthened.

Each Xuthilian saw himself walking behind the glare of a strong torch down a long straight marble passageway, through a high vaulted corridor of seamless stone. Cobwebs and the dust of centuries stirred softly beneath his feet, and the air was musty with the scent of long-dead years. A torch swung toward the roof of the passageway, and its beam was lost in the vast reaches of the chamber above.

Then the passage widened into a great amphitheatre—a tremendous room that dwarfed to insignificance the wide Xuthilian forum. Telepathically each viewer saw himself—as Tul had done—press forward on eager feet, then stop and swing his flaring torch around the strangest sight a living eye had ever seen. Rows upon rows of recessed drawers, bronze-plated and embossed with hieroglyphs—these were the content of the curious cube. These and nothing more.

The picture wavered, faded. The thoughts of Tul replaced it, communicating directly with each watcher.

"Undeniably there is some great mystery yet to be dissolved concerning the curious cube. What these drawers contain we do not know. Archives, perhaps, of some long-vanished race. But it will take long years of arduous labor with the finest of modern equipment to open even *one* of the mighty shelves. Their gigantic size and intricate construction defies us. If living creatures built the curious cube—and we may suppose they did—their bodily structure was on a scale so vastly greater than our own that we are utterly unable to comprehend the purpose of their instruments. Only one thing found in the cube was in any way comparable to machinery we know and employ."

Tul turned and nodded to two of his assistants. They moved forward, staggering under the weight of a huge stone slab, circular in form, set into a greater square of some strange fibroid material. Attached to this giant dais was a huge resilient hawser, larger in width by half than those who bore it.

"The cable attached to this slab," continued Tul, "is very long. It reaches all the way into the heart of the curious cube. Obviously it has some bearing on the secret, but what that bearing is, we do not know. Our engineers will have to dismember the slab to solve its meaning. As you see, it is solid—"

Tul stepped upon the stone. . . .

And as Tul stepped upon the push-button, quiescent current flowed from reservoirs dormant for ages, and from the dark depths of the curious cube an electrically controlled recorder spoke.

"Men—" said a human voice—"men of the fiftieth century—we, your brothers of the twenty-fifth need you. For humanity's sake, we call on you for help.

"As I speak, our solar system is plunging into a great chlorine cloud from which it will not emerge for hundreds of years. All mankind is doomed to destruction. In this specially constructed vault we have laid to rest ten thousand of the greatest minds of Earth, hermetically sealed to sleep in an induced catalepsy until the fiftieth century. By that time the danger will be ended.

"The door to our vault at last has opened. If there be men alive, and if the air be pure, pull down the lever beside the portal of our tomb and we will waken.

"If no man hear this plea—if no man still be alive—then farewell, world. The sleeping remnants of the race of man sleep on forever."

"Solid," repeated Tul. "Yet, as you see, it seems to yield slightly." He continued dubiously, "Citizens of Xuthil, we are as baffled by this mystery as you are. But you may rest assured that your council of scientists will make every effort to solve it."

The green glare of the *menavisors* faded. Xuthil, perplexed and marveling, returned to its daily labors. On street corners and in halls, in homes and offices, Xuthilians briefly paused to touch antennae, discussing the strange wonder.

For the voice from the curious cube had not been heard by any living creature. Sole rulers of the fiftieth century were ants—and ants cannot hear.

## Questions for Students to Discuss

1. What assumptions did the creators of the curious cube make when selecting the format their message was contained in?
2. What assumptions did the ants make when attempting to unlock the mysteries of the curious cube?
3. Think about the process used to create the message in the curious cube. Who do you think created the message (an individual, an organization, a committee)? Do you think they were politicians, scientists, athletes, or something else? How do you think they decided on the content of the message and other information in the cube (quickly by an individual or slowly through a rigorous process debated by many)?

4. Imagine you could understand the message in the curious cube. Why would or wouldn't you trust it? How would you be sure that the message was from an official individual or group? To what extent does the format and delivery mode indicate the message was from an official or trustworthy source?

5. In this story, humans from the twenty-fifth century attempt to communicate to humans in the fiftieth century. How does one communicate that far into the future? Do some research on how the U.S. Department of Energy (DOE) proposes to communicate to people ten thousand years into the future about keeping away from nuclear (radioactive) waste. In what ways do the DOE's efforts remind you of the "The Voice from the Curious Cube"? In what ways is the DOE adhering to the "Information Creation As a Process" frame?

6. When it comes to the selection of information formats and modes of delivery, what is the point of this story? In one sentence, summarize it.

## *THE KING* BY ALAN M. CVANCARA

The bull tyrannosaurus senses his imminent death this sunny Creta-ceous morning. Arthritis pains his neck and right hip, and his stomach rumbles from not having eaten for 3 days. His younger brethren now seize choice prey.

He yawns, stretches, raises his ailing bulk with difficulty to full height. The tyrannosaurus shuffles along the bottom of a valley lush with cycadeoids, cycads, ginkgoes, conifers, and ferns.

He leans against a cycad to rest. A movement in the shadows cap-tures his attention. Another rustle stirs the undergrowth, and this time he thrills at the sight in clear view: a triceratops calf—easy pickings!

He summons his remaining energy reserves to pursue the terrified quarry. The tyrannosaurus glimpses a flash of larger movement to his right. The calf's mother charges her child's attacker from a clump of cycadeoids; her protective mother's fury knows no bounds. She thunders toward the tyrannosaurus, thrusts her horns into the predator, and gores his midsection again and again. In his weakened condition, the tyrannosaurus can't parry her vicious jabs, and experiences—for the first time—a hapless victim's vulnerability.

The mighty predator rolls on his side. He wheezes from punctured lungs, winces at the pain from multiple flesh wounds and broken ribs. With a satisfied grunt, the mother struts off to retrieve her child—her bony shield drenched in tyrannosaurus blood.

The tyrannosaurus suffers into the late afternoon. Just before death, he bites into the unbearable pain in his ribs. One of his 6-inch teeth, loosened in earlier battles, embeds in his pebbled hide. Early that eve-ning, a thunderstorm floods the valley and sweeps the tyrannosaurus' carcass into a nearby oxbow lake where it settles to the bottom, be-comes entombed in mud.

Sixty-five million years after *all* the dinosaurs die, a paleontologist stands over an almost complete, well-articulated tyrannosaurus skeleton exposed in a bed of shale. A tyrannosaurus tooth lies against the rib cage, its source socket hidden from view on the underside of the skull.

The paleontologist expounds to his student excavation crew: "We have here the magnificent skeleton of a tyrannosaurus, specifically *Ty-rannosaurus rex*, king of the Cretaceous flesh-eating dinosaurs. The evidence is clear. It's obvious from the broken ribs and associated tyrannosaurus tooth, that our animal battled with another tyrannosaurus—and lost. It's likely, too, that these animals were cannibalistic."

The crew members nod in agreement, aim complimentary smiles at their omniscient leader.

One of the male graduate students, though, steeped in scientific approaches, questions the paleontologist. "Can we be sure that another tyrannosaurus inflicted the mortal wounds? Our fossil seems to be of an old individual."

The paleontologist wrinkles his forehead at someone questioning his explanation. "I'd agree with you on that—so?"

"Then maybe the separated tooth belongs to our fossil, and dropped out because of old age. The empty socket for the tooth could be hidden on the underside of the skull."

The paleontologist sighs. "That's a big maybe."

The graduate student continues. "It also seems possible to me that a triceratops, with its impressive horns, could have delivered the necessary stabs and blows to break the tyrannosaurus' ribs. Not that the triceratops necessarily initiated an attack, but became combative in self-defense. Or, possibly a case of a mother defending her young."

The paleontologist shakes his head. "What you say is interesting. But experience with dinosaurs tells me that I'm probably correct." He scans the rest of the excavation crew. "Any other comments or questions?"

## Questions for Students to Discuss

1. If the paleontologists in "The King" were only able to examine digital images of the Tyrannosaurus rex fossil rather than the actual fossil or a 3D model of the fossil, how might this shape their perception of the cause of the dinosaur's death? What type of information can you get from an actual fossil that you can't get from a digital image? What types of analysis can you do with a digital image of a fossil that you can't with an actual fossil?

2. What other sources of information might a paleontologist use to learn about dinosaurs? Why do or don't you believe that these sources are as valuable as a fossil in understanding the topic?

3. How might the paleontologists in this story share their fossil find with other paleontologists?

4. What is a reason that using a fossil to learn about dinosaurs would be better than using a book?

5. When interpreting the meaning of the fossil regarding the Tyrannosaurus rex's death, the professor and graduate student reach different conclusions. How do their power relations enter into the process of research, creating, revising, and disseminating information about the fossil?

6. What do you think is the main point of this story in terms of the "Information Creation As a Process" frame?

# 3

# INFORMATION HAS VALUE

The next three stories, grouped under the "Information Has Value" frame, encourage you to think about the economic, legal, and social importance of information in different contexts.

In "The Censors," Luisa Valenzuela tells the story of a man who works in a government department that censors personal letters. As the story progresses, he changes in a profound way. The story raises questions about the nature and control of information in a society as well as our individual responsibility to comply with or contest the practices concerning the value of information.

Paul Theroux's "The Memory Priest of the Creech People" introduces us to a society of hill-dwelling aboriginals in south-central Sumatra where the notion of information is quite different than ours. Theroux's story invites us to consider the ways our understanding of the social issues surrounding the use and access of information is culturally constructed.

In "The People Who Owned the Bible," Will Shetterly tells a tale of copyright abuse gone wild. Shetterly takes an extreme position on copyright ownership in order to ridicule it. His story raises questions about the economic value of information, fair use, and the limitations of owning intellectual property, as well as the social implications that can result from favoring the owners of copyrighted works.

The "Information Has Value" frame in textbox 3.1 provides a starting point for you to think about these issues.

Textbox 3.1
**Information Has Value**

**Information possesses several dimensions of value, including as a commodity, as a means of education, as a means to influence, and as a means of negotiating and understanding the world. Legal and socioeconomic interests influence information production and dissemination.**

The value of information is manifested in various contexts, including publishing practices, access to information, the commodification of personal information, and intellectual property laws. The novice learner may struggle to understand the diverse values of information in an environment where "free" information and related services are plentiful and the concept of intellectual property is first encountered through rules of citation or warnings about plagiarism and copyright law. As creators and users of information, experts understand their rights and responsibilities when participating in a community of scholarship. Experts understand that value may be wielded by powerful interests in ways that marginalize certain voices. However, value may also be leveraged by individuals and organizations to effect change and for civic, economic, social, or personal gains. Experts also understand that the individual is responsible for making deliberate and informed choices about when to comply with and when to contest current legal and socioeconomic practices concerning the value of information.

**Knowledge Practices**

Learners who are developing their information literate abilities

- give credit to the original ideas of others through proper attribution and citation;
- understand that intellectual property is a legal and social construct that varies by culture;
- articulate the purpose and distinguishing characteristics of copyright, fair use, open access, and the public domain;
- understand how and why some individuals or groups of individuals may be underrepresented or systematically marginalized within the systems that produce and disseminate information;

- recognize issues of access or lack of access to information sources;
- decide where and how their information is published;
- understand how the commodification of their personal information and online interactions affects the information they receive and the information they produce or disseminate online;
- make informed choices regarding their online actions in full awareness of issues related to privacy and the commodification of personal information.

## Dispositions

Learners who are developing their information literate abilities

- respect the original ideas of others;
- value the skills, time, and effort needed to produce knowledge;
- see themselves as contributors to the information marketplace rather than only consumers of it;
- are inclined to examine their own information privilege.

## THE CENSORS BY LUISA VALENZUELA (TRANSLATED BY DAVID UNGER)

Poor Juan! One day they caught him with his guard down before he could even realize that what he had taken as a stroke of luck was really one of fate's dirty tricks. These things happen the minute you're careless and you let down your guard, as one often does. Juancito let happiness—a feeling you can't trust—get the better of him when he received from a confidential source Mariana's new address in Paris and he knew that she hadn't forgotten him. Without thinking twice, he sat down at his table and wrote her a letter. *The* letter that keeps his mind off his job during the day and won't let him sleep at night (what had he scrawled, what had he put on that sheet of paper he sent to Mariana?).

Juan knows there won't be a problem with the letter's contents, that it's irreproachable, harmless. But what about the rest? He knows that they examine, sniff, feel, and read between the lines of each and every letter, and check its tiniest comma and most accidental stain. He knows that all letters pass from hand to hand and go through all sorts of tests in the huge censorship offices and that, in the end, very few continue on their way. Usually it takes months, even years, if there aren't any snags; all this time the freedom, maybe even the life, of both sender and receiver is in jeopardy. And that's why Juan's so down in the dumps: thinking that something might happen to Mariana because of his letters. Of all people, Mariana, who must finally feel safe there where she always dreamed she'd live. But he knows that the *Censor's Secret Command* operates all over the world and cashes in on the discount in air rates; there's nothing to stop them from going as far as that hidden Paris neighborhood, kidnapping Mariana, and returning to their cozy homes, certain of having fulfilled their noble mission.

Well, you've got to beat them to the punch, do what everyone tries to do: sabotage the machinery, throw sand in its gears, get to the bottom of the problem so as to stop it.

This was Juan's sound plan when he, like many others, applied for a censor's job—not because he had a calling or needed a job: no, he applied simply to intercept his own letter, a consoling but unoriginal idea. He was hired immediately, for each day more and more censors are needed and no one would bother to check on his references.

Ulterior motives couldn't be overlooked by the *Censorship Division*, but they needn't be too strict with those who applied. They knew how hard it would be for those poor guys to find the letter they wanted and even if they did, what's a letter or two when the new censor would snap up so many others? That's how Juan managed to join the *Post Office's Censorship Division*, with a certain goal in mind.

The building had a festive air on the outside which contrasted with its inner staidness. Little by little, Juan was absorbed by his job and he felt at peace since he was doing everything he could to get his letter for Mariana. He didn't even worry when, in his first month, he was sent to *Section K* where envelopes are very carefully screened for explosives.

It's true that on the third day, a fellow worker had his right hand blown off by a letter, but the division chief claimed it was sheer negligence on the victim's part. Juan and the other employees were allowed to go back to their work, albeit feeling less secure. After work, one of them tried to organize a strike to demand higher wages for unhealthy work, but Juan didn't join in; after thinking it over, he reported him to his superiors and thus got promoted.

You don't form a habit by doing something once, he told himself as he left his boss's office. And when he was transferred to *Section J*, where letters are carefully checked for poison dust, he felt he had climbed a rung in the ladder.

By working hard, he quickly reached *Section E* where the work was more interesting, for he could now read and analyze the letters' contents. Here he could even hope to get hold of his letter which, judging by the time that had elapsed, had gone through the other sections and was probably floating around in this one.

Soon his work became so absorbing that his noble mission blurred in his mind. Day after day he crossed out whole paragraphs in red ink, pitilessly chucking many letters into the censored basket. These were horrible days when he was shocked by the subtle and conniving ways employed by people to pass on subversive messages; his instincts were so sharp that he found behind a simple "the weather's unsettled" or "prices continue to soar" the wavering hand of someone secretly scheming to overthrow the Government.

His zeal brought him swift promotion. We don't know if this made him happy. Very few letters reached him in *Section B*—only a handful passed the other hurdles—so he read them over and over again, passed them under a magnifying glass, searched for microprint with an electronic microscope, and tuned his sense of smell so that he was beat by the time he made it home. He'd barely manage to warm up his soup, eat some fruit, and fall into bed, satisfied with having done his duty. Only his darling mother worried, but she couldn't get him back on the right road. She'd say, though it wasn't always true: Lola called, she's at the bar with the girls, they miss you, they're waiting for you. Or else she'd leave a bottle of red wine on the table. But Juan wouldn't overdo it: any distraction could make him lose his edge and the perfect censor had to be alert, keen, attentive, and sharp to nab cheats. He had a truly patriotic task, both self-denying and uplifting.

His basket for censored letters became the best fed as well as the most cunning basket in the whole *Censorship Division*. He was about to congratulate himself for having finally discovered his true mission, when his letter to Mariana reached his hands. Naturally, he censored it without regret. And just as naturally, he couldn't stop them from executing him the following morning, another victim of his devotion to his work.

## Questions for Students to Discuss

1. According to the *Wex Legal Dictionary*, "intellectual property is any product of the human mind that the law protects from unauthorized use by others." Why do or don't you agree that the ideas in Juan's letter are his property? Do you think people can—or should—own ideas? What are the implications of owning or not owning ideas? When answering, think richly in terms of the economic, civic, social, legal, and personal implications.

2. At first, Juan contests the government's legal right to censor the mail. Later he complies with it. Indeed, he becomes one of the government's most skilled and productive censors. How do you account for his shifting perspective? When and why did he flip? What implications does this have for your perspective on intellectual property, copyright, and fair use? Why might you, for example, illegally download copyrighted movies at one stage of your life but work diligently to prevent illegal copying and downloading of movies at another?

3. In this story Juan censors print mail. If he were working in today's technology-rich environment, what other type of material could he censor?

4. Who decides where and how information is distributed in this story? Who decides where and how information is published in your society?

5. Does the government ever have a legitimate reason to obtain and censor an individual's information? What questions would you ask yourself to determine whether you should comply with or contest your government's censorship practices?

6. What are the important lessons that can be inferred about the value of information?

## THE MEMORY PRIEST OF THE CREECH PEOPLE BY PAUL
THEROUX

One person alone, always a man, serves as the memory for all the dates and names and events of the Creech, the hill-dwelling aboriginals of south-central Sumatra. This person possesses an entire history of the people and may spend as much as a week, day and night, reciting the various genealogies.

This Memory Priest reminds the Creech of who they are and what they have done. He is their entertainment and their historian, their memory and mind and imagination. He keeps the Creech amused and informed. The Creech have no chief or headman. The Memory Priest serves as the sole authority.

The Memory Priest is awarded his title at birth. As soon as he is able to talk he is given to understand that he is the repository of all the Creech lore.

His is not an easy career. He must memorize great lists of family names and must be able to recite all the events that took place from the moment of his birth.

The Creech are mostly placid, though they are subject to odd fits of violence. Biting themselves in order to show remorse is not unknown, and clawing their own faces is common. They are also untruthful and unreliable, prone to thieving, gossiping, gambling, and sudden spasms of the most aggressive behavior.

What the Memory Priest knows, the immensity of his storehouse of facts, is nothing compared with the one fact that he does not know, a secret that is withheld from him: After thirty years have passed, and he is old by Creech standards (possibly toothless, almost certainly wrinkled and shrunken), a meeting is convened. He recites the Creech history, and at the conclusion of this he is put to death. He is finally roasted and eaten by every member of the Creech, in a ritual known as the Ceremony of Purification.

The next male child born to a Creech woman is designated Memory Priest and elevated; history begins once again. Nothing that has taken place before his birth has any reality, all quarrels are settled, all debts nullified.

So the Memory Priest, now an infant, soon a man, learns his role, believing that history begins with him and never aware that at a specified moment his life will end. Yet it is the death of the Memory Priest that the Creech people live for and whisper about, the wiping out of all debts, all crimes, all shame and failure. They eagerly anticipate the amnesia his death will bring. Throughout his life, though he is unaware of it, he is less a supreme authority than a convenient receptacle into which all the ill-assorted details of the Creech are tossed. Secretly, he is mocked for not knowing that it will all end in oblivion, at the time of his certain death.

## Questions for Students to Discuss

1.  According to the "Information Has Value" frame, "information possesses several dimensions of value, including as a commodity, as a means of education, and as a means of negotiating and understanding the world." What value does information have in this story?

2.  The "Information Has Value" frame argues that we must "give credit to the original idea of others through the proper attribution and citation." However, the story takes place in an indigenous society. Information is memorized and passed orally in Creech society (rather than written and cited). Further, traditional knowledge is conceived of and owned collectively (rather than individually). How can you remake the "give credit to the original idea of others through the proper attribution and citation" knowledge practice to recognize and protect the value of information in indigenous societies like the Creech? If you believe the frame has irreconcilable differences with Creech cultural practices, how might you change the frame to recognize those differences?

3.  Since the Memory Priest plays such a great role in the Creech's information practices, should he know as a young man that he will be killed at age thirty and consumed by the community in the Ceremony of Purification? To what degree does his lack of awareness and subsequent lack of consent weaken the civic, social, and personal gains of the value of the information that his death provides? What practices are there in your society where people are not fully aware that the information they produce is being used to promote someone else's civic, economic, social, or personal gains?

4. To what extent do you believe members of Creech culture see themselves as contributors to knowledge rather than only as users of it? How about yourself? To what degree do you think of yourself as a contributor to the information marketplace or a consumer of information in your society?
5. How does lack of access to Creech history from multiple sources both benefit and harm individuals and groups in Creech culture?
6. What do you think is the main point of "The Memory Priest of the Creech People" in terms of the "Information Has Value" frame?

## THE PEOPLE WHO OWNED THE BIBLE BY WILL SHETTERLY

It was time for another Mickey Mouse Copyright Extension to keep Disney's star property out of the public domain. Somebody's nephew had a bright idea. Instead of telling Congress to add the standard twenty years to the length of copyright, why not go for the big time? Extend copyright by 500 years.

Somebody's niece added a smarter reason: A 500 year extension would let Disney track down Shakespeare's heirs and buy all rights to the Bard. No matter how much the heirs wanted, the deal would pay for itself in no time. Every school that ever wanted to perform or study Shakespeare would have to send a check to Disney. Every newspaper or magazine or radio show that wanted to quote the Bard would have to send one, too. So Disney asked, and Congress gave, and the World Intellectual Property Organization followed Congress's example. Disney paid off Shakespeare's heirs, then used the Shakespeare profits to buy all rights from the heirs of Dumas, Dickens, Twain, Mary Shelley, Jane Austen, Bram Stoker and more. Once most of the films in every other studio's library were subject to Disney's copyright, they went bankrupt or became divisions of Disney.

And everyone was content, except for the storytellers who had to buy a Disney license or prove their work owed nothing to the last 500 years of literature.

Then Jimmy Joe Jenkins's DNA proved he was the primary descendent of the translators of the King James Version of the Bible. At first, Jimmy was satisfied with ten percent of the price of every KJV sold and 10 percent of every collection plate passed by any church that used the KJV. But when some churches switched to newer translations, Jimmy sicced his lawyers on all translations based on the KJV. That got him a cut of every Bible and every Christian service in English. Some translators claimed their work was based on older versions and should therefore be exempt, but none of them could afford to fight Jimmy in court.

So the churches grumbled and paid Jimmy his tithe, except for the Mormons, Christian Scientists, Seventh Day Adventists, Quakers, and Unitarian Universalists. Jimmy said their teachings hurt the commercial value of his property and refused to let them use the Bible. All of those groups dissolved, except for the Unitarian Universalists, who didn't notice a change.

Then Jimmy took out the parts of the Bible that criticized rich people. Most of the surviving major churches didn't notice that. But they did complain when Jimmy changed the traditional translations of Yusuf and Miryam to Jimmy Joe and Lulabelle, the name of his pretty new wife.

But when his Lulabelle ran off with a Bible salesman, Jimmy retired to one of his mansions and refused to let anyone print any more Bibles or use the Bible in any way that raised money.

The surviving churches sent delegates to Disney, begging them to get Congress to shorten the copyright period to put the KJV back in the public domain. But Disney had picked up the rights to a Restoration revenge tragedy that looked like a great vehicle for Britney Spears, so they made a counteroffer.

Congress extended copyright for an additional two thousand years, and the WIPO followed their example. Jimmy had to pay every dollar he had made to the Catholic Church, because the KJV was based on St. Jerome's Vulgate version. In order to use the Bible, all Protestants became Catholic. Disney bought the copyrights and trademarks for Robin Hood, King Arthur, and the Arabian Nights.

And everyone was content, except for the storytellers who had to buy a Disney license or prove their work owed nothing to the last two thousand years of myth and folklore.

Then Spike Greenbaum's DNA proved she was the primary descendent of Jesus or his brother James. Spike agreed to let Catholics use their Bible after the Pope married her to her girlfriend. Then she said that since Catholic priests could be married or celibate for the first thousand years, then had to be celibate for the next thousand, now all priests should be married to at least one other person. And since Jesus had told his followers to sell their goods and give their money to the poor, every expensive thing owned by the Church had to be given up for AIDS research.

Catholics grumbled, but they took some satisfaction when the courts ruled that the Qur'an was a derivative work, and Spike would not let Saudi Arabia use it until they ruled that women could drive cars and men could not.

The Pope considered recreating the church of Mithra, which would let his people keep worshipping on Sundays and celebrating a virgin birth on December 25th. But his wives pointed out that Rome's Mithra

Cult fell within the current period of copyright, and the primary heir was a charter member of NAMBLA who was preparing legal action against Spike for the rights to the Bible. So the Catholics sent delegates to Disney, begging them to shorten the copyright period to put Jesus's words in the public domain.

But Disney had just picked up the rights to the Satyricon, which looked like a great vehicle for Ashton Kutcher, so they made a counteroffer.

Congress extended copyright an additional twenty-five hundred years. Spike Greenbaum owed every dollar she had made to Israel, because St. Jerome's translation was based on Hebrew sacred texts. To use the Bible, all Catholics became Jewish, and Disney bought the rights to the Iliad and the Odyssey.

And everyone was content, except for the storytellers who had to buy a Disney license or prove their work did not owe anything to any story that had ever been part of human civilization.

Then Kurosh Jadali's DNA proved he was the primary descendent of Zarathushtra, whose teachings about monotheism had been adopted by the Jews during the Babylonian Captivity. Kurosh said that since Zoroaster had taught religious tolerance, he would be glad to let the Jews use their sacred texts. In return, he only wanted a thousand Euros for each Torah that was published and three-fourths of any money that flowed through a synagogue. When the rabbis grumbled, Kurosh asked if they were communists who didn't respect intellectual property.

So all the branches of Judaism sent delegates to Disney, begging them to roll back the period of copyright so that Zarathushtra's teachings would be in the public domain. But Disney had picked up the rights to the Epic of Gilgamesh, which looked like a great vehicle for Jim Carrey, so they made a counteroffer.

Congress extended copyright for an additional hundred thousand years. Kurosh Jadali had to give all his money to the United Nations, since everyone's DNA proved they were the descendants of the first people to tell stories about gods. Disney bought the rights to a story that had been painted on a wall about some people with some animals that they thought would be a great vehicle for Mel Gibson.

And everyone was content, except for the storytellers who had to buy a Disney license or prove their work did not owe anything to any story that had characters doing anything.

Until one day a woman came into the Disney offices and said thanks to the extension of the period of copyright law, patent law had been extended, too. And since her DNA proved she was the primary descendent of the first person who cast shadows on a wall and told stories about them, she would like to speak to the C.E.O. about every movie and television show that Disney had thought it owned.

## Questions for Students to Discuss

1. How does the title of this story, "The People Who Owned the Bible," make you feel? Does it, for instance, disturb, amuse, or interest you? Why do you feel this way?

2. Why do you or don't you believe that the Bible (or any other holy book such as the Torah or Koran) is too valuable or important for any one person or organization to own? What, if anything, is distinctively different about these holy books that make individual ownership problematic?

3. Why does Disney want to extend the Mickey Mouse copyright as well as buy the rights to Shakespeare's works? What value does this information have?

4. The story suggests that all intellectual works are prompted by, draw on, or written in reaction to previous works. In other words, every author can trace his or her ideas back to another author that came before him or her. To what extent do you agree with this? What does this say about an author's ability to have an original idea? Further, if every work is a derivative, a creative response, or a reassembly, critique, or extension of previous works, what does this mean for copyright?

5. If an individual or organization owned the Bible, the Torah, or the Qur'an, when, if at all, do you think clergy (e.g., priests, ministers, rabbis, or imams) should comply with and when should they should contest copyright law regulating their use of these holy books?

6. What is the moral of this story in terms of the "Information Has Value" frame?

# 4

# RESEARCH AS INQUIRY

In the "Research As Inquiry" frame, research is described as *iterative*. An iterative process is a repetitive one. An effective researcher arrives at his or her conclusion only after repeated rounds of research. Each round of research leads to new findings and in turn new questions. The answers to these new questions often lead to the development of the research question. As the stories in this chapter illustrate, the need to research goes beyond the library and the classroom, beyond school papers and assignments.

"A Fable" by Robert Fox helps us gain insight about iterative research by providing us an example of what it isn't when a young man and woman make an important life decision in a matter of minutes on an early morning subway ride. Implicit in this story is that the need to research has a connection to personal life and is not merely an academic activity.

"College Queen" by William Brandon is about a college professor who makes assumptions and conclusions about his students (and himself) that are not based on sound research or reasons. His experiences with students work against him in the story and he fails to ask new and increasingly complex questions about those he encounters. Although much of the action takes place in a college setting, the need for research is largely personal and professional.

"To Serve Man" by Damon Knight provides us with a compelling social need for research when people encounter and interact with creatures from outer space that land on Earth. Despite this need, we see yet another example of the failure to realize the complexity and tenacity required of thorough and critical research as well as the dramatic consequences. Knight's story also raises political questions about what we choose not to ask and why, particularly in good economic times.

These stories serve as an introduction to the "Research As Inquiry" frame in textbox 4.1.

Textbox 4.1

**Research As Inquiry**

**Research is iterative and depends upon asking increasingly complex or new questions whose answers in turn develop additional questions or lines of inquiry in any field.**

Experts see inquiry as a process that focuses on problems or questions in or between disciplines that are open or unresolved. Experts recognize the collaborative effort within a discipline to extend the knowledge in that field. Many times, this process includes points of disagreement wherein debate and dialogue work to deepen the conversations around knowledge. This process of inquiry extends beyond the academic world to the community at large, and the process of inquiry may focus upon personal, professional, or societal needs. The spectrum of inquiry ranges from asking simple questions that depend upon basic recapitulation of knowledge to increasingly sophisticated abilities to refine research questions, use more advanced research methods, and explore more diverse disciplinary perspectives. Novice learners acquire strategic perspectives on inquiry and a greater repertoire of investigative methods.

**Knowledge Practices**

Learners who are developing their information literate abilities

- formulate questions for research based on information gaps or on reexamination of existing, possibly conflicting, information;
- determine an appropriate scope of investigation;
- deal with complex research by breaking complex questions into simple ones, limiting the scope of investigations;
- use various research methods based on need, circumstance, and type of inquiry;

- monitor gathered information and assess for gaps or weaknesses;
- organize information in meaningful ways;
- synthesize ideas gathered from multiple sources;
- draw reasonable conclusions based on the analysis and interpretation of information.

## Dispositions

Learners who are developing their information literate abilities

- consider research as open-ended exploration and engagement with information;
- appreciate that a question may appear to be simple but still may be disruptive and important to research;
- value intellectual curiosity in developing questions and learning new investigative methods;
- maintain an open mind and a critical stance;
- value persistence, adaptability, and flexibility, and recognize that ambiguity can benefit the research process;
- seek multiple perspectives during information gathering and assessment;
- seek appropriate help when needed;
- follow ethical and legal guidelines in gathering and using information;
- demonstrate intellectual humility (i.e., recognize their own intellectual or experiential limitations).

## *A FABLE* BY ROBERT FOX

The young man was clean shaven and neatly dressed. It was early Monday morning and he got on the subway. It was the first day of his first job and he was slightly nervous; he didn't know exactly what his job would be. Otherwise he felt fine. He loved everybody he saw. He loved everybody on the street and everybody disappearing into the subway, and he loved the world because it was a fine clear day and he was starting his first job.

Without kicking anybody, the young man was able to find a seat on the Manhattan-bound train. The car filled quickly and he looked up at the people standing over him envying his seat. Among them were a mother and daughter who were going shopping. The daughter was a beautiful girl with blond hair and soft-looking skin, and he was immediately attracted to her.

"He's staring at you," the mother whispered to the daughter.

"Yes, Mother, I feel so uncomfortable. What shall I *do*?"

"He's in love with you."

"In love with me? How can you tell?"

"Because I'm your mother."

"But what shall I do?"

"Nothing. He'll try to talk to you. If he does, answer him. Be nice to him. He's only a boy."

The train reached the business district and many people got off. The girl and her mother found seats opposite the young man. He continued to look at the girl who occasionally looked to see if he was looking at her.

The young man found a good pretext for standing and giving his seat to an elderly man. He stood over the girl and her mother. They whispered back and forth and looked up at him. At another stop the seat next to the girl was vacated, and the young man blushed but quickly took it.

"I knew it," the mother said between her teeth. "I knew it, I *knew* it."

The young man cleared his throat and tapped the girl. She jumped.

"Pardon me," he said. "You're a very pretty girl."

"Thank you," she said.

"Don't talk to him," her mother said. "Don't answer him. I'm warning you. Believe me."

"I'm in love with you," he said to the girl.

"I don't believe you," the girl said.

"Don't answer him," the mother said.

"I really do," he said. "In fact, I'm so much in love with you that I want to marry you."

"Do you have a job?" she said.

"Yes, today is my first day. I'm going to Manhattan to start my first day of work."

"What kind of work will you do?" she asked.

"I don't know exactly," he said. "You see, I didn't start yet."

"It sounds exciting," she said.

"It's my first job, but I'll have my own desk and handle a lot of papers and carry them around in a briefcase, and it will pay well, and I'll work my way up."

"I love you," she said.

"Will you marry me?"

"I don't know. You'll have to ask my mother."

The young man rose from his seat and stood before the girl's mother. He cleared his throat very carefully for a long time. "May I have the honor of having your daughter's hand in marriage?" he said, but he was drowned out by the subway noise.

The mother looked up at him and said, "What?" He couldn't hear her either, but he could tell by the movement of her lips and by the way her face wrinkled up that she said, What.

The train pulled to a stop.

"May I have the honor of having your daughter's hand in marriage!" he shouted, not realizing there was no subway noise. Everybody on the train looked at him, smiled, and then they all applauded.

"Are you crazy?" the mother asked.

The train started again.

"What?" he said.

"Why do you want to marry her?" she asked.

"Well, she's pretty—I mean, I'm in love with her."

"Is that all?"

"I guess so," he said. "Is there supposed to be more?"

"No. Not usually," the mother said. "Are you working?"

"Yes. As a matter of fact, that's why I'm going into Manhattan so early. Today is the first day of my first job."

"Congratulations," the mother said.

"Thanks," he said. "Can I marry your daughter?"

"Do you have a car?" she asked.

"Not yet," he said. "But I should be able to get one pretty soon. And a house, too."

"A house?"

"With lots of rooms."

"Yes, that's what I expected you to say," she said. She turned to her daughter. "Do you love him?"

"Yes, Mother, I do."

"Why?"

"Because he's good, and gentle, and kind."

"Are you sure?"

"Yes."

"Then you really love him."

"Yes."

"Are you sure there isn't anyone else that you might love and might want to marry?"

"No, Mother," the girl said.

"Well, then," the mother said to the young man. "Looks like there's nothing I can do about it. Ask her again."

The train stopped.

"My dearest one," he said, "will you marry me?"

"Yes," she said.

Everybody in the car smiled and applauded.

"Isn't life wonderful?" the boy asked the mother.

"Beautiful," the mother said.

The conductor climbed down from between the cars as the train started up and, straightening his dark tie, approached them with a solemn black book in his hand.


## Questions for Students to Discuss

1. Using the "Research As Inquiry" frame as a guide, in what ways does finding a husband or wife differ from finding information for a course assignment, for example? Before answering, make

sure to consider the myriad of tools available to help you find love and spouses on the Internet.

2. Explain why you do or don't agree that the characters in "A Fable" should have asked increasingly complex and new questions as they received answers to their questions.

3. Does the daughter consult with anyone in her search? Does the young man? Why was or wasn't this consultation adequate? Who else should they have consulted with before making their decision? Why? Why is or isn't it adequate to make such a personal decision by yourself without assistance from others? Is the same true for research for a school assignment?

4. In "A Fable," the characters meet, fall in love, and marry within the course of a few minutes. Why do or don't you agree that this was an adequate amount of time to make this decision? In other words, was the search thorough? Explain how one might know how much information is enough in order to know when one is in love and should marry someone. Now think about research for a school assignment. Explain when you know how much research is enough.

5. If you were asked to continue the story in divorce court a year after the couple married, describe the questions you think the judge would ask the couple about what went wrong and how it happened.

6. What important lessons from this story can be applied to research in your life and your schoolwork?

## COLLEGE QUEEN BY WILLIAM BRANDON

Dr. Todentanz elevated himself a time or two on his toes and fixed his eyes on the paneled ceiling in his favorite lecture-room attitude. He said, "To the superior intellect the mass man is always utterly predictable. That is one of the basic principles of my teaching."

The class opened notebooks and thirty sweatered backs bent to scribble.

Dr. Todentanz was thinking, as he often did, that the undergraduates before him represented the mass man and he himself, naturally, the superior intellect. He was entertaining himself by establishing, even this early in the term, the utter predictability of each of them. The two boys and the blonde girl in the center of the front row, for example: there was a pattern to be read at a glance.

The girl was extraordinarily pretty. She had a nice smile and sea-blue eyes (in which, Dr. Todentanz thought poetically, Ariel would be wont to sparkle). Her casual skirt and cardigan had probably cost more than an associate professor made in six weeks. She was the young who would inherit the earth and find it delightful. Dr. Todentanz thought of her, almost without irony, as The Girl Who Would Always Have Everything.

The young man on her right was clearly a big-man-on-the-campus type, fraternity president, varsity halfback, and the owner of a yellow convertible. Dr. Todentanz mentally named him Big Pupil. It was plain that Big Pupil was actively interested in promoting a close acquaintance with The Girl Who Would Always Have Everything. It was utterly predictable that, being Big Pupil, he would manage this small matter with ease and dispatch.

The lanky student on the left of The Girl Who Would Always Have Everything was also deep in dreams of her, Dr. Todentanz had observed, but in his case prediction need not hesitate in awarding a quick blank. A grim lad, grinding out the last year of his GI degree, he was hopelessly distant from the Greek-letter life of Big Pupil and The Girl Who Would Always Have Everything. He was certain to remain a disappointed worshiper from afar.

He was traveling under the added handicap, Dr. Todentanz happened to know, of a war orphan he had quixotically adopted in France, a little girl who was now nine years old and attending the elementary school operated by the university in connection with the College of

Education. To support this rather absurd responsibility he worked several hours a day in the faculty restaurant and several hours a night in a local laundry. Dr. Todentanz gave him the title of Earnest Quixote.

Earnest Quixote would sooner or later attempt some stumbling overture toward The Girl Who Would Always Have Everything, but it would fail. It would win him nothing but embarrassment, and afterward Big Pupil and The Girl Who Would Always Have Everything would laugh about it together and then forget the incident completely.

As the first weeks of the term passed, Dr. Todentanz was pleased to see his predictions working out with their usual accuracy.

Big Pupil seized his opportunity to shine in the eyes of The Girl Who Would Always Have Everything on an occasion when the professor had turned some remark of hers with a particularly witty reply. The class guffawed, and Dr. Todentanz got lost for a time in a lengthy pause of self-appreciation, for he enjoyed savoring these small triumphs. The silence had stretched into a minute or so when Big Pupil said impulsively, "Am I writing too fast for you, Professor?"

Dr. Todentanz was able to forgive him because he understood Big Pupil's intention of presenting himself, by that wisecrack, as the gallant defender of The Girl Who Would Always Have Everything. He was not surprised to see them later that day walking under the elms holding hands.

Earnest Quixote was some time longer in building up to his forlorn pitch. It was an extravagant gesture, dramatic in a desperate way and unhappily corny, much as Dr. Todentanz had anticipated.

It took place on the afternoon that Psychology 108 spent in the college elementary school, studying the children there. A fourth-grade teacher, asking her charges to tell the people what they wanted most in all the world, called upon the dark-eyed little girl, Jeanne, who was Earnest Quixote's child of charity. It developed that Jeanne did not want a puppy dog or a kitty cat or even a bicycle, which last Dr. Todentanz knew to be a red-hot lie, as Jeanne had admired his own bike with wistful longing on more than one occasion.

The teacher said, "Then won't you tell us what it is you do want, dear? There must be something you secretly wish for above everything else."

"I want a mother to go with my father," Jeanne said. She pointed at Earnest Quixote. "That's my father there, only not really, but he's sort of my father, and he's very nice."

Earnest Quixote turned red.

"I see," the teacher said. "And you want a mother, too."

"I want one awfully bad," Jeanne said. "But I want a nice one. Maybe one like her." This time Jeanne pointed at The Girl Who Would Always Have Everything.

The class giggled and Big Pupil grinned patronizingly and Earnest Quixote turned white.

"She looks like she'd go good with my father," Jeanne said. "I think she'd go very well with him."

The class howled happily, the teacher dismissed Jeanne, and Dr. Todentanz declared the day's session at an end.

Earnest Quixote, wretched with embarrassment, went to The Girl Who Would Always Have Everything and said, "Look, can I drop dead or something?"

The Girl Who Would Always Have Everything smiled and said, "Well, no, but it's nice of you to offer." She was not captivated or offended, but only amused, all as Dr. Todentanz had foreseen.

But the professor was intrigued enough by the little girl's part in this patently put-up job to look for her later on the school grounds. He found her starting to ride away on a shiny new bicycle.

"Ah," Dr. Todentanz said, "a present!"

"I just got it today," Jeanne said. "That's why I said I didn't want a bicycle, because now I've got one."

Not far away, Dr. Todentanz saw Earnest Quixote and The Girl Who Would Always Have Everything on a bench. Earnest Quixote was talking with great seriousness. Now the lame apology, Dr. Todentanz thought, the embarrassed silence, and the next stop would be his swift consignment to outer darkness, as far as the girl was concerned.

"Could it be," Dr. Todentanz suggested craftily, "that somebody gave you that bicycle for saying what you said today about wanting a mother?"

"I'm not supposed to tell," Jeanne said.

"But it was a gift from someone, eh?"

"Well, yes."

Dr. Todentanz indicated Earnest Quixote on the bench. "Him?"

"Oh, goodness no," Jeanne said, astonished at his unworldliness. "Her."

## Questions for Students to Discuss

1. Do you agree that intellectual humility is a characteristic of a good researcher? Using evidence from the story, why do or don't you believe that Dr. Todentanz demonstrated intellectual humility? How might a researcher's lack of intellectual humility affect the soundness of his or her conclusions?

2. If some of the characters charged Dr. Todentanz with unethical behavior, who might they be and why? Was any aspect of Dr. Todentanz's behavior unethical?

3. If Dr. Todentanz had spoken with other characters or researchers earlier and throughout the story, how might that have shaped his conclusions? Why do or don't you agree that good researchers seek multiple perspectives when conducting and interpreting their work?

4. What conclusion can you reach about the relationship between the method of research and the soundness of conclusion?

5. What part does research play in this story? Why do or don't you agree that any of the characters performed research?

6. Summarize the meaning of the story as it pertains to the "Research As Inquiry" frame.

## TO SERVE MAN BY DAMON KNIGHT

The Kanamit were not very pretty, it's true. They looked something like pigs and something like people, and that is not an attractive combination. Seeing them for the first time shocked you; that was their handicap. When a thing with the countenance of a fiend comes from the stars and offers a gift, you are disinclined to accept.

I don't know what we expected interstellar visitors to look like—those who thought about it at all, that is. Angels, perhaps, or something too alien to be really awful. Maybe that's why we were all so horrified and repelled when they landed in their great ships and we saw what they really were like.

The Kanamit were short and very hairy—thick, bristly brown-gray hair all over their abominably plump bodies. Their noses were snoutlike and their eyes small, and they had thick hands of three fingers each. They wore green leather harnesses and green shorts, but I think the shorts were a concession to our notions of public decency. The garments were quite modishly cut, with slash pockets and half-belts in the back. The Kanamit had a sense of humor, anyhow.

There were three of them at this session of the U.N., and, lord, I can't tell you how queer it looked to see them there in the middle of a solemn plenary session—three fat piglike creatures in green harness and shorts, sitting at the long table below the podium, surrounded by the packed arcs of delegates from every nation. They sat correctly upright, politely watching each speaker. Their flat ears drooped over the earphones. Later on, I believe, they learned every human language, but at this time they knew only French and English.

They seemed perfectly at ease—and that, along with their humor, was a thing that tended to make me like them. I was in the minority; I didn't think they were trying to put anything over.

The delegate from Argentina got up and said that his government was interested in the demonstration of a new cheap power source, which the Kanamit had made at the previous session, but that the Argentine government could not commit itself as to its future policy without a much more thorough examination.

It was what all the delegates were saying, but I had to pay particular attention to Señor Valdes, because he tended to sputter and his diction was bad. I got through the translation all right, with only one or two momentary hesitations, and then switched to the Polish-English line to hear how Grigori was doing with Janciewicz. Janciewicz was the cross Grigori had to bear, just as Valdes was mine.

Janciewicz repeated the previous remarks with a few ideological variations, and then the Secretary-General recognized the delegate from France, who introduced Dr. Denis Lévêque, the criminologist, and a great deal of complicated equipment was wheeled in.

Dr. Lévêque remarked that the question in many people's minds had been aptly expressed by the delegate from the U.S.S.R. at the preceding session, when he demanded, "What is the motive of the Kanamit? What is their purpose in offering us these unprecedented gifts, while asking nothing in return?"

The doctor then said, "At the request of several delegates and with the full consent of our guests, the Kanamit, my associates and I have made a series of tests upon the Kanamit with the equipment which you see before you. These tests will now be repeated."

A murmur ran through the chamber. There was a fusillade of flash-bulbs, and one of the TV cameras moved up to focus on the instrument board of the doctor's equipment. At the same time, the huge television screen behind the podium lighted up, and we saw the blank faces of two dials, each with its pointer resting at zero, and a strip of paper tape with a stylus point resting against it.

The doctor's assistants were fastening wires to the temples of one of the Kanamit, wrapping a canvas-covered rubber tube around his fore-arm, and taping something to the palm of his right hand.

In the screen, we saw the paper tape begin to move while the stylus traced a slow zigzag pattern along it. One of the needles began to jump rhythmically; the other flipped halfway over and stayed there, wavering slightly.

"These are the standard instruments for testing the truth of a state-ment," said Dr. Lévêque. "Our first object, since the physiology of the Kanamit is unknown to us, was to determine whether or not they react to these tests as human beings do. We will now repeat one of the many experiments which were made in the endeavor to discover this."

He pointed to the first dial. "This instrument registers the subject's heartbeat. This shows the electrical conductivity of the skin in the palm of his hand, a measure of perspiration, which increases under stress. And this—" pointing to the tape-and-stylus device—"shows the pattern

and intensity of the electrical waves emanating from his brain. It has
been shown, with human subjects, that all these readings vary markedly
depending upon whether the subject is speaking the truth."

He picked up two large pieces of cardboard, one red and one black.
The red one was a square about three feet on a side; the black was a
rectangle three and a half feet long. He addressed himself to the Kanama.

"Which of these is longer than the other?"

"The red," said the Kanama.

Both needles leaped wildly, and so did the line on the unrolling tape.

"I shall repeat the question," said the doctor. "Which of these is
longer than the other?"

"The black," said the creature.

This time the instruments continued in their normal rhythm.

"How did you come to this planet?" asked the doctor.

"Walked," replied the Kanama.

Again the instruments responded, and there was a subdued ripple of
laughter in the chamber.

"Once more," said the doctor. "How did you come to this planet?"

"In a spaceship," said the Kanama, and the instruments did not
jump.

The doctor again faced the delegates. "Many such experiments were
made," he said, "and my colleagues and myself are satisfied that the
mechanisms are effective. Now—" he turned to the Kanama—"I shall
ask our distinguished guest to reply to the question put at the last
session by the delegate of the U.S.S.R.—namely, what is the motive of
the Kanamit people in offering these great gifts to the people of Earth?"

The Kanama rose. Speaking this time in English, he said, "On my
planet there is a saying, 'There are more riddles in a stone than in a
philosopher's head.' The motives of intelligent beings, though they may
at times appear obscure, are simple things compared to the complex
workings of the natural universe. Therefore I hope that the people of
Earth will understand, and believe, when I tell you that our mission
upon your planet is simply this—to bring you the peace and plenty
which we ourselves enjoy, and which we have in the past brought to
other races throughout the galaxy. When your world has no more hunger, no more war, no more needless suffering, that will be our reward."

And the needles had not jumped once.

The delegate from the Ukraine jumped to his feet, asking to be recognized, but the time was up and the Secretary-General closed the session.

I met Grigori as we were leaving the chamber. His face was red with excitement. "Who promoted that circus?" he demanded.

"The tests looked genuine to me," I told him.

"A circus!" he said vehemently. "A second-rate farce! If they were genuine, Peter, why was debate stifled?"

"There'll be time for debate tomorrow, surely."

"Tomorrow the doctor and his instruments will be back in Paris. Plenty of things can happen before tomorrow. In the name of sanity, man, how can anybody trust a thing that looks as if it ate the baby?"

I was a little annoyed. I said, "Are you sure you're not more worried about their politics than their appearance?"

He said, "Bah," and went away.

The next day reports began to come in from government laboratories all over the world where the Kanamit's power source was being tested. They were wildly enthusiastic. I don't understand such things myself, but it seemed that those little metal boxes would give more electrical power than an atomic pile, for next to nothing and nearly forever. And it was said that they were so cheap to manufacture that everybody in the world could have one of his own. In the early afternoon there were reports that seventeen countries had already begun to set up factories to turn them out.

The next day the Kanamit turned up with plans and specimens of a gadget that would increase the fertility of any arable land by 60 to 100 per cent. It speeded the formation of nitrates in the soil, or something. There was nothing in the newscasts any more but stories about the Kanamit. The day after that, they dropped their bombshell.

"You now have potentially unlimited power and increased food supply," said one of them. He pointed with his three-fingered hand to an instrument that stood on the table before him. It was a box on a tripod, with a parabolic reflector on the front of it. "We offer you today a third gift which is at least as important as the first two."

He beckoned to the TV men to roll their cameras into closeup position. Then he picked up a large sheet of cardboard covered with drawings and English lettering. We saw it on the large screen above the podium; it was clearly legible.

"We are informed that this broadcast is being relayed throughout your world," said the Kanama. "I wish that everyone who has equipment for taking photographs from television screens would use it now."

The Secretary-General leaned forward and asked a question sharply, but the Kanama ignored him.

"This device," he said, "generates a field in which no explosive, of whatever nature, can detonate."

There was uncomprehending silence.

The Kanama said, "It cannot now be suppressed. If one nation has it, all must have it." When nobody seemed to understand, he explained bluntly, "There will be no more war."

That was the biggest news of the millennium, and it was perfectly true. It turned out that the explosions the Kanama was talking about even included gasoline and Diesel explosions. They had simply made it impossible for anybody to mount or equip a modern army.

We could have gone back to bows and arrows, of course, but that wouldn't have satisfied the military. Besides, there wouldn't be any reason to make war. Every nation would soon have everything.

Nobody ever gave another thought to those lie-detector experiments, or asked the Kanamit what their politics were. Grigori was put out; he had nothing to prove his suspicions.

I quit my job at the U.N. a few months later, because I foresaw that it was going to die under me anyhow. U.N. business was booming at the time, but after a year or so there was going to be nothing for it to do. Every nation on Earth was well on the way to being completely self-supporting; they weren't going to need much arbitration.

I accepted a position as translator with the Kanamit Embassy, and it was there I ran into Grigori again. I was glad to see him, but I couldn't imagine what he was doing there.

"I thought you were on the opposition," I said. "Don't tell me you're convinced the Kanamit are all right."

He looked rather shamefaced. "They're not what they look, anyhow," he said.

It was as much of a concession as he could decently make, and I invited him down to the embassy lounge for a drink. It was an intimate kind of place, and he grew confidential over the second daiquiri.

"They fascinate me," he said. "I hate them instinctively still—that hasn't changed—but I can evaluate it. You were right, obviously; they mean us nothing but good. But do you know—" he leaned across the table—"the question of the Soviet delegate was never answered."

I am afraid I snorted.

"No, really," he said. "They told us what they wanted to do—'to bring to you the peace and plenty which we ourselves enjoy.' But they didn't say *why*."

"Why do missionaries—"

"Missionaries be damned!" he said angrily. "Missionaries have a religious motive. If these creatures have a religion, they haven't once mentioned it. What's more, they didn't send a missionary group; they sent a diplomatic delegation—a group representing the will and policy of their whole people. Now just what have the Kanamit, as a people or a nation, got to gain from our welfare?"

I said, "Cultural—"

"Cultural cabbage soup! No, it's something less obvious than that, something obscure that belongs to their psychology and not to ours. But trust me, Peter, there is no such thing as a completely disinterested altruism. In one way or another, they have something to gain."

"And that's why you're here," I said. "To try to find out what it is."

"Correct. I wanted to get on one of the ten-year exchange groups to their home planet, but I couldn't; the quota was filled a week after they made the announcement. This is the next best thing. I'm studying their language, and you know that language reflects the basic assumptions of the people who use it. I've got a fair command of the spoken lingo already. It's not hard, really, and there are hints in it. Some of the idioms are quite similar to English. I'm sure I'll get the answer eventually."

"More power," I said, and we went back to work.

I saw Grigori frequently from then on, and he kept me posted about his progress. He was highly excited about a month after that first meeting; said he'd got hold of a book of the Kanamit's and was trying to puzzle it out. They wrote in ideographs, worse than Chinese, but he was determined to fathom it if it took him years. He wanted my help.

Well, I was interested in spite of myself, for I knew it would be a long job. We spent some evenings together, working with material from Kanamit bulletin boards and so forth, and with the extremely limited English-Kanamit dictionary they issued to the staff. My conscience bothered me about the stolen book, but gradually I became absorbed

by the problem. Languages are my field, after all. I couldn't help being
fascinated.

We got the title worked out in a few weeks. It was *How to Serve
Man*, evidently a handbook they were giving out to new Kanamit members of the embassy staff. They had new ones in, all the time now, a
shipload about once a month; they were opening all kinds of research
laboratories, clinics and so on. If there was anybody on Earth besides
Grigori who still distrusted those people, he must have been somewhere in the middle of Tibet.

It was astonishing to see the changes that had been wrought in less
than a year. There were no more standing armies, no more shortages,
no unemployment. When you picked up a newspaper you didn't see *H-
Bomb* or *Satellite* leaping out at you; the news was always good. It was a
hard thing to get used to. The Kanamit were working on human bio-
chemistry, and it was known around the embassy that they were nearly
ready to announce methods of making our race taller and stronger and
healthier—practically a race of supermen—and they had a potential
cure for heart disease and cancer.

I didn't see Grigori for a fortnight after we finished working out the
title of the book; I was on a long-overdue vacation in Canada. When I
got back, I was shocked by the change in his appearance.

"What on Earth is wrong, Grigori?" I asked. "You look like the very
devil."

"Come down to the lounge."

I went with him, and he gulped a stiff Scotch as if he needed it.

"Come on, man, what's the matter?" I urged.

"The Kanamit have put me on the passenger list for the next exchange ship," he said. "You, too, otherwise I wouldn't be talking to you."

"Well," I said, "but—"

"They're not altruists."

I tried to reason with him. I pointed out they'd made Earth a para-
dise compared to what it was before. He only shook his head.

Then I said, "Well, what about those lie-detector tests?"

"A farce," he replied, without heat. "I said so at the time, you fool.
They told the truth, though, as far as it went."

"And the book?" I demanded, annoyed. "What about that—*How to
Serve Man*? That wasn't put there for you to read. They *mean* it. How
do you explain that?"

"I've read the first paragraph of that book," he said. "Why do you suppose I haven't slept for a week?"

I said, "Well?" and he smiled a curious, twisted smile.

"It's a cookbook," he said.

## Questions for Students to Discuss

1. When discussing the lie-detector tests with the narrator (Peter), Grigori says, "They told the truth, though, as far as it went." The narrator adds, "Nobody ever gave another thought to those lie-detector experiments, or asked the Kanamit what their politics were." Why didn't more human beings ask the Kanama increasingly complex or new questions to get a more complete picture of their intentions? What does this suggest about the problems of posing a single question in your research?

2. The Kanama is subjected to a lie-detector experiment to determine the Kanamit's motivation for bringing peace and prosperity to the people of Earth. To what extent was the incorrect assessment of the truth of the Kanama's answers a result of the method used or the questions asked? How does this story illustrate the need for various research methods based on need, circumstance, and type of inquiry? How does it illustrate the need to carefully formulate questions for research?

3. When attempting to learn the Kanamit language, Grigori turns to the narrator (Peter) for help. To what extent did Grigori seek out the appropriate help? Who might he have asked instead of or in addition to the narrator? Why might these people have been better partners in decoding and translating the Kanamit language?

4. Throughout the story, Grigori persists in his disbelief of the Kanamit's selfless concern for the well-being of the people of Earth. Even as life got better for human beings, he doubted Kanamit altruism. The ACRL framework argues that learners who are developing their information skills should "maintain an open mind and a critical stance." They also argue that they should "value persistence, adaptability, and flexibility." Why do or don't you agree that Grigori exhibited these dispositions? How did Grigori's

dispositions help or hurt his efforts to research and understand the Kanamit language?

5. Grigori and the narrator (Peter) steal a Kanamit book to translate. Why was or wasn't it morally acceptable for them to violate ethical or legal guidelines in their research?

6. What does this story teach us about the importance of "asking increasingly complex or new questions whose answers in turn develop additional questions of lines of inquiry" when conducting research?

# 5

# SCHOLARSHIP AS CONVERSATION

Research is a social process. Scholars do not simply perform experiments or examinations by themselves in their offices or laboratories. They are part of a community; they communicate with each other. One way that they do this is through publications such as academic journals. The articles in an academic journal are often prompted by or in response to previous studies and articles. In this sense, like a conversation, they are part of an exchange of thoughts and information. If you examine a wide range of articles, you will notice that research differs across the disciplines. A dance scholar's approach is very different from an astronomer's approach. When you do research, you are entering into this exchange of ideas and information with the other members of that disciplinary community. In order to participate in research and add something new, you need to find out what has been said. The next three stories help us reflect on the "Scholarship As Conversation" frame.

"An Old Man" by Guy de Maupassant is about a senior citizen who has an obsessive fear of death. His phobia leads him to frequent conversations with his doctor about the causes and conditions of the recently deceased in his town. The old man, though, is quick to make pronouncements about the causes of death rather than seeking out his doctor's opinion. Thus the old man has no new insight or discoveries as a result of these exchanges.

In "Charles," Shirley Jackson tells a story about a kindergartner who provides his parents with regular reports about a mischievous classmate's behavioral problems. Despite their concern about what is happening in the classroom and how this is affecting their son, the parents fail to investigate the details or look at any evidence beyond their son's testimony. This story encourages us to consider the wisdom of accepting one uncontested perspective or version of events from a familiar or trusted source.

Mack Reynolds's story "Mind over Mayhem" presents the limitations of using a rapid, individual, and unsystematic method of character assessment when a stranger enters a bar shortly before closing time and interacts with the bartender and the remaining customer. By comparing and contrasting the process of scholarly conversation with the individual method used in this story, the reader obtains a better understanding of the importance of scholarly exchange and the benefits of the collective nature of scholarship.

The stories in this section illustrate the "Scholarship As Conversation" frame in textbox 5.1.

Textbox 5.1
**Scholarship As Conversation**
**Communities of scholars, researchers, or professionals engage in sustained discourse with new insights and discoveries occurring over time as a result of varied perspectives and interpretations.**

Research in scholarly and professional fields is a discursive practice in which ideas are formulated, debated, and weighed against each other over extended periods of time. Instead of seeking discrete answers to complex problems, experts understand that a given issue may be characterized by several competing perspectives as part of an ongoing conversation in which information users and creators come together and negotiate meaning. Experts understand that although some topics have established answers through this process, a query may not have a single uncontested answer. Experts are therefore inclined to seek out many perspectives, not merely the ones with which they are familiar. These perspectives might be in their own discipline or profession or may be in other fields. Though novice learners and experts at all levels can take part in the conversation, established power and authority structures may influence their ability to participate and can privilege certain voices and information. Developing familiarity with the sources of evidence, methods, and modes of discourse in the field assists novice learners to enter the conversation. New forms of scholarly and research conversations provide more avenues in which a wide variety of individuals may have a voice in the conversation. Providing attribution to relevant previous research is also an obligation of participation in the conversation. It enables the conversation to move forward and strengthens one's voice in the conversation.

**Knowledge Practices**

Learners who are developing their information literate abilities

- cite the contributing work of others in their own information production;
- contribute to scholarly conversation at an appropriate level, such as local online community, guided discussion, undergraduate research journal, conference presentation/poster session;
- identify barriers to entering scholarly conversation via various venues;
- critically evaluate contributions made by others in participatory information environments;
- identify the contribution that particular articles, books, and other scholarly pieces make to disciplinary knowledge;
- summarize the changes in scholarly perspective over time on a particular topic within a specific discipline;
- recognize that a given scholarly work may not represent the only or even the majority perspective on the issue.

**Dispositions**

Learners who are developing their information literate abilities

- recognize they are often entering into an ongoing scholarly conversation and not a finished conversation;
- seek out conversations taking place in their research area;
- see themselves as contributors to scholarship rather than only consumers of it;
- recognize that scholarly conversations take place in various venues;

- suspend judgment on the value of a particular piece of scholarship until the larger context for the scholarly conversation is better understood;
- understand the responsibility that comes with entering the conversation through participatory channels;
- value user-generated content and evaluate contributions made by others;
- recognize that systems privilege authorities and that not having a fluency in the language and process of a discipline disempowers their ability to participate and engage.

## *AN OLD MAN* BY GUY DE MAUPASSANT (TRANSLATED BY FRANCIS STEEGMULLER)

All the newspapers had carried the advertisement:

"The new watering place of Rondelis offers all desired advantages for a long stay and even for permanent residence. Its ferruginous waters, recognized as the best in the world for counteracting all impurities of the blood, seem also to possess particular qualities calculated to prolong human life. This singular circumstance is perhaps due in part to the exceptional situation of the town, which lies surrounded by mountains and in the very center of a pine forest. For several centuries it has been celebrated for numerous cases of extraordinary longevity."

And the public came in droves.

One morning the doctor in charge of the springs was asked to call on a new arrival, Monsieur Daron, who had come to Rondelis only a few days before and had rented a charming villa on the edge of the forest. He was a little old man of eighty-six, still sprightly, wiry, healthy, active, who went to infinite pains to conceal his age.

He asked the doctor to be seated, and immediately questioned him: "Doctor, if I am well, it is thanks to hygienic living. I am not very old, but have reached a certain age, and I keep free of all illnesses, all indisposition, even the slightest discomfort, by means of hygiene. I am told that the climate of this place is very favorable for the health. I am very willing to believe it, but before establishing myself here I want proof. I am therefore going to ask you to call on me once a week, to give me, very exactly, the following information:

"I wish first of all to have a complete, utterly complete, list of all the inhabitants of the town and surroundings who are more than eighty years old. I also need a few physical and physiological details concerning each. I wish to know their professions, their kinds of life, their habits. Each time one of these people dies, you will inform me, indicating the precise cause of death, as well as the circumstances."

Then he graciously added: "I hope, Doctor, that we may become good friends," and he stretched out his wrinkled little hand. The doctor took it, promising his devoted co-operation.

M. Daron had always had a strange fear of death. He had deprived himself of almost all the pleasures because they are dangerous, and whenever anyone expressed surprise that he did not drink wine—wine, that bringer of fancy and gaiety—he replied in a voice containing a note of fear: "I value my life." And he pronounced *My*, as if that life, *His* life, possessed some generally unknown value. He put into that *My* such a difference between his life and the life of others, that no answer was possible.

Indeed, he had a very particular way of accentuating the possessive pronouns designating all the parts of his person or even things belonging to him. When he said "My eyes, my legs, my arms, my hands," it was clear that no mistake must be made: those organs did not belong to everyone. But this distinction was particularly noticeable when he spoke of his physician: "My doctor." One would have said that this doctor was his, only his, destined for him alone, to take care of his illnesses and nobody else's, and that he was superior to all doctors in the universe, all, without exception.

He had never considered other men except as kinds of puppets, created as furniture for the natural world. He divided them into two classes: those whom he greeted because some chance had put him in contact with them, and those whom he did not greet. Both categories of individuals were to him equally insignificant.

But beginning with the day when the doctor of Rondelis brought him the list of the seventeen inhabitants of the town who were over eighty, he felt awaken in his heart a new interest, an unfamiliar solicitude for these old people whom he was going to see fall by the wayside one after the other.

He had no desire to make their acquaintance, but he had a very clear idea of their persons, and with the doctor, who dined with him every Thursday, he spoke only of them. "Well, doctor, how is Joseph Poincot today? We left him a little ill last week." And when the doctor had given him the patient's bill of health M. Daron proposed modifications in diet, experiments, methods of treatment which he might later apply to himself if they succeeded with the others. The seventeen old people were an experimental field from which much was to be learned.

One evening the doctor came in and announced: "Rosalie Tournel is dead." M. Daron shuddered and immediately demanded, "What of?" "Of an angina." The little old man uttered an "ah" of relief. Then he declared: "She was too fat, too big; she must have eaten too much. When I get to her age, I'll be more careful." (He was two years older than Rosalie, but never admitted to be over seventy.)

A few months later, it was the turn of Henri Brissot. M. Daron was very moved. This time it was a man—thin, within three months of his own age, and very prudent. He dared ask for no details, but waited anxiously for the doctor to tell him. "Ah, he died suddenly, just like that? He was very well last week. He must have done something unwise, Doctor." The doctor, who was enjoying himself, replied, "I believe not. His children told me he was very careful."

Then, no longer able contain himself M. Daron demanded, with anguish, "But . . . but . . . What did he die of, then?"

"Of pleurisy."

That was joyful news, really joyful. The little old man clapped his dry hands. "I knew it! I told you he had done something unwise. Pleurisy doesn't come just by itself. He took a breath of fresh air after his dinner, and the cold lodged on his chest. Pleurisy! That is an accident, not an illness. Only crazy men die of pleurisy."

And he ate his dinner gaily, talking of those who remained. "There are only fifteen now, but they are all strong, aren't they? All of life is like that, the weakest fall first; people who go beyond thirty have a good chance to reach sixty; those who pass sixty often get to eighty; and those who pass eighty almost always reach the century mark, because they are the most robust, the most careful, the most hardened."

Still two others disappeared during the year, one of dysentery and the other of a choking fit. M. Daron derived a great deal of amusement from the death of the former, and concluded that he must have eaten something exciting the day before. "Dysentery is the disease of the imprudent; you should have watched over his hygiene, Doctor." As for the choking fit, it could only have come from a heart condition, hitherto unrecognized.

But one evening the doctor announced the passing of Paul Timonet, a kind of mummy, of whom it had been hoped to make a centenarian, a living advertisement for the watering place. When M. Daron asked, as usual, "What did he die of?" the doctor replied, "Really, I don't know."

"What do you mean, you don't know? One always knows. Wasn't there some organic lesion?"

The doctor shook his head. "No, none."

"Perhaps some infection of the liver or the kidneys?"

"No—they were perfectly sound."

"Did you observe whether the stomach functioned regularly? A stroke is often caused by bad digestion."

"There was no stroke."

M. Daron, very perplexed, became excited. "But he certainly died of something! What is your opinion?"

The doctor raised his arms. "I absolutely do not know. He died because he died, that's all."

Then M. Daron, in a voice full of emotion, demanded: "Exactly how old was that one? I can't remember."

"Eighty-nine."

And the little old man, with an air at once incredulous and reassured, cried, "Eighty-nine! So, it wasn't old age! . . ."

## Questions for Students to Discuss

1. When examining complex problems, expert researchers often "seek out many perspectives, not merely the ones with which they are familiar." To what degree did Monsieur Daron do this when examining the cause of death of the aged in his town?

2. When discussing the cause of death of the senior citizens, why would or wouldn't you describe Monsieur Daron's exchanges with his doctor as scholarly conversations? Why? What characteristics do scholarly conversations have that other conversation types lack?

3. Presumably Monsieur Daron's doctor is an authority on medical matters. Yet Monsieur Daron debated his doctor's conclusions on medical matters regularly. Indeed he felt he knew more than his doctor. So why doesn't Monsieur Daron privilege his doctor's determinations on the cause of death in the older residents? To what degree should he? Although he does not have a medical degree, why should or shouldn't he participate and debate the doctor on his assessments?

4. Monsieur Daron and his doctor speak openly about other people's health and cause of death. Is this appropriate? Why should or shouldn't doctors have conversations, scholarly or otherwise, about their patients' medical information (even after their death)? Can you think of any circumstances in which the disclo-

sure of a deceased person's medical records should be the focus of scholarly conversation?

5. At the end of the story, Monsieur Daron's doctor does not know the cause of death of an eighty-nine-year-old man. Frustrated with his doctor's inability to pinpoint the cause of death, Monsieur Daron, an eighty-six-year-old man who believes that human longevity can be controlled by "careful living," concludes "it wasn't old age." Do some research on dying of old age. Throughout history, have scholars and doctors believed one could die of old age? What about contemporary scholars and doctors? Do you see any indications of shifts or debates in perspective over time?

6. What do you think are the lessons from this story in terms of the "Scholarship As Conversation" frame?

## *CHARLES* BY SHIRLEY JACKSON

The day my son Laurie started kindergarten he renounced corduroy overalls with bibs and began wearing blue jeans with a belt. I watched him go off the first morning with the older girl next door, seeing clearly that an era of my life was ended, my sweet-voiced nursery-school tot replaced by a long-trousered, swaggering character who forgot to stop at the corner and wave good-bye to me.

He came home the same way, the front door slamming open, his hat on the floor, and the voice suddenly become raucous shouting, "Isn't anybody *here*?"

At lunch he spoke insolently to his father, spilled his baby sister's milk, and remarked that his teacher said we were not to take the name of the Lord in vain.

"How *was* school today?" I asked, elaborately casual.

"All right," he said.

"Did you learn anything?" his father asked.

Laurie regarded his father coldly. "I didn't learn nothing," he said.

"Anything," I said. "Didn't learn anything."

"The teacher spanked a boy, though," Laurie said, addressing his bread and butter. "For being fresh," he added, with his mouth full.

"What did he do?" I asked. "Who was it?"

Laurie thought. "It was Charles," he said, "He was fresh. The teacher spanked him and made him stand in a corner. He was awfully fresh."

"What did he do?" I asked again, but Laurie slid off his chair, took a cookie, and left, while his father was still saying, "See here, young man."

The next day Laurie remarked at lunch, as soon as he sat down, "Well, Charles was bad again today." He grinned enormously and said, "Today Charles hit the teacher."

"Good heavens," I said, mindful of the Lord's name. "I suppose he got spanked again?"

"He sure did," Laurie said. "Look up," he said to his father.

"What?" his father said, looking up.

"Look down," Laurie said. "Look at my thumb. Gee, you're dumb." He began to laugh insanely.

"Why did Charles hit the teacher?" I asked quickly.

"Because she tried to make him color with red crayons," Laurie said. "Charles wanted to color with green crayons so he hit the teacher and she spanked him and said nobody play with Charles but everybody did."

The third day—it was Wednesday of the first week—Charles bounced a see-saw on the head of a little girl and made her bleed, and the teacher made him stay inside all during recess. Thursday Charles had to stand in a corner during story-time because he kept pounding his feet on the floor. Friday Charles was deprived of blackboard privileges because he threw chalk.

On Saturday I remarked to my husband, "Do you think kindergarten is too unsettling for Laurie? All this toughness and bad grammar, and this Charles boy sounds like such a bad influence."

"It'll be all right," my husband said reassuringly. "Bound to be people like Charles in the world. Might as well meet them now as later."

On Monday Laurie came home late, full of news. "Charles," he shouted as he came up the hill; I was waiting anxiously on the front steps. "Charles," Laurie yelled all the way up the hill, "Charles was bad again."

"Come right in," I said, as soon as he came close enough. "Lunch is waiting."

"You know what Charles did?" he demanded, following me through the door. "Charles yelled so in school they sent a boy in from first grade to tell the teacher she had to make Charles keep quiet, and so Charles had to stay after school. And so all the children stayed to watch him."

"What did he do?" I asked.

"He just sat there," Laurie said, climbing into his chair at the table. "Hi, Pop, y'old dust mop."

"Charles had to stay after school today," I told my husband. "Everyone stayed with him."

"What does this Charles look like?" my husband asked Laurie. "What's his other name?"

"He's bigger than me," Laurie said. "And he doesn't have any rubbers and he doesn't ever wear a jacket."

Monday night was the first Parent-Teachers meeting, and only the fact that the baby had a cold kept me from going; I wanted passionately to meet Charles's mother. On Tuesday Laurie remarked suddenly, "Our teacher had a friend come to see her in school today."

"Charles's mother?" my husband and I asked simultaneously.

"Naaah," Laurie said scornfully. "It was a man who came and made us do exercises, we had to touch our toes. Look." He climbed down from his chair and squatted down and touched his toes. "Like this," he said. He got solemnly back into his chair and said, picking up his fork, "Charles didn't even *do* exercises."

"That's fine," I said heartily. "Didn't Charles want to do the exercises?"

"Naaah," Laurie said. "Charles was so fresh to the teacher's friend he wasn't *let* do exercises."

"Fresh again," I said.

"He kicked the teacher's friend," Laurie said. "The teacher's friend told Charles to touch his toes like I just did and Charles kicked him."

"What are they going to do about Charles, do you suppose?" Laurie's father asked him.

Laurie shrugged elaborately. "Throw him out of school, I guess," he said.

Wednesday and Thursday were routine; Charles yelled during story hour and hit a boy in the stomach and made him cry. On Friday Charles stayed after school again and so did all the other children.

With the third week of kindergarten Charles was an institution in our family; the baby was being a Charles when he filled his wagon full of mud and pulled it through the kitchen; even my husband, when he caught his elbow in the telephone cord and pulled telephone, ashtray, and a bowl of flowers off the table, said, after the first minute, "Looks like Charles."

During the third and fourth weeks it looked like a reformation in Charles; Laurie reported grimly at lunch on Thursday of the third week, "Charles was so good today the teacher gave him an apple."

"What?" I said, and my husband added warily, "You mean Charles?"

"Charles," Laurie said. "He gave the crayons around and he picked up the books afterward and the teacher said he was her helper."

"What happened?" I asked incredulously.

"He was her helper, that's all," Laurie said, and shrugged.

"Can this be true, about Charles?" I asked my husband that night. "Can something like this happen?"

"Wait and see," my husband said cynically. "When you've got a Charles to deal with, this may mean he's only plotting."

He seemed to be wrong. For over a week Charles was the teacher's helper; each day he handed things out and he picked things up; no one had to stay after school.

"The PTA meeting's next week again," I told my husband one evening. "I'm going to find Charles's mother there."

"Ask her what happened to Charles," my husband said. "I'd like to know."

"I'd like to know myself," I said.

On Friday of that week things were back to normal. "You know what Charles did today?" Laurie demanded at the lunch table, in a voice slightly awed. "He told a little girl to say a word and she said it and the teacher washed her mouth out with soap and Charles laughed."

"What word?" his father asked unwisely, and Laurie said, "I'll have to whisper it to you, it's so bad." He got down off his chair and went around to his father. His father bent his head down and Laurie whispered joyfully. His father's eyes widened.

"Did Charles tell the little girl to say *that*?" he asked respectfully.

"She said it *twice*," Laurie said. "Charles told her to say it *twice*."

"What happened to Charles?" my husband asked.

"Nothing," Laurie said. "He was passing out the crayons."

Monday morning Charles abandoned the little girl and said the evil word himself three or four times, getting his mouth washed out with soap each time. He also threw chalk.

My husband came to the door with me that evening as I set out for the PTA meeting. "Invite her over for a cup of tea after the meeting," he said. "I want to get a look at her."

"If only she's there," I said prayerfully.

"She'll be there," my husband said. "I don't see how they could hold a PTA meeting without Charles's mother."

At the meeting I sat restlessly, scanning each comfortable matronly face, trying to determine which one hid the secret of Charles. None of them looked to me haggard enough. No one stood up in the meeting and apologized for the way her son had been acting. No one mentioned Charles.

After the meeting I identified and sought out Laurie's kindergarten teacher. She had a plate with a cup of tea and a piece of chocolate cake; I had a plate with a cup of tea and a piece of marshmallow cake. We maneuvered up to one another cautiously, and smiled.

"I've been so anxious to meet you," I said. "I'm Laurie's mother."

"We're all so interested in Laurie," she said.

"Well, he certainly likes kindergarten," I said. "He talks about it all the time."

"We had a little trouble adjusting, the first week or so," she said primly, "but now he's a fine little helper. With occasional lapses of course."

"Laurie usually adjusts very quickly," I said. "I suppose this time it's Charles's influence."

"Charles?"

"Yes," I said, laughing, "you must have your hands full in that kindergarten, with Charles."

"Charles?" she said. "We don't have any Charles in the kindergarten."

## Questions for Students to Discuss

1. Expert researchers are "inclined to seek out many perspectives, not merely the ones with which they are familiar." To what extent do the characters in Jackson's story exhibit this behavior?

2. Why didn't Laurie's parents look into the details of his reports about Charles?

3. When you stand back and look at Laurie's claims about Charles and the evidence he used, you can see how weak his argument is. At what point in the story, though, did you arrive at this conclusion? When did you judge Laurie (the source) as credible? When did you arrive at the conclusion that Charles was a problem student? Why did or didn't you suspend judgment until the end of the story when the larger context for Laurie's depiction of Charles was better understood? What is the moral of the story and what are the implications for your own research?

4. The story takes place over the course of a school year. Over time, Laurie and his parents talk about Charles. To what degree did Laurie's parents, though, become experts on Charles? To what degree were they able to speak about Charles with greater sophistication and complexity as the story progressed?

5. Where (in what places) did the conversations about Charles take place? If they had taken place in more or different venues, do you

believe Laurie's parents would have asked more and different questions?

6. What is the moral of this story in relation to the "Scholarship As Conversation" frame?

## *MIND OVER MAYHEM* BY MACK REYNOLDS

The others had straggled out one by one and I was the only remaining customer. The bartender drifted down and wiped the bar in front of me listlessly, and yawned.

"Why the hell don't you go home, Jerry?" he asked conversationally.

I put the tabloid I'd been glancing at to one side and grinned at him. "Haven't got a home, Sam; just a hotel room with four walls and a bed and a chair or two and a couple hundred pocket books. I'd rather sit here and look at you."

He leaned on the bar before me and said, "You oughta get married, Jerry. Why don't you ask that girl . . . what was her name? The blonde, pretty little girl."

"Frances."

"Yeah, that's right. Frances. Why don't you ask her to marry you?"

I twisted my glass on the bar, lifted it over to a new spot, twisted it again and then again, making small wet circles.

"I did," I said. "A couple of months ago I asked her, 'Why don't we get married, Frances?'"

"Well, what'd she say?" Sam asked, yawning again.

"She just laughed and said, 'Who'd have either of us, Jerry?'"

Sam snorted. "I've heard that one before."

"It's almost two o'clock. You can't expect me to be original this time of night."

A guy came in and took a stool two down from me and Sam walked over to him.

"Only fifteen minutes to go," Sam said. "What'll it be?"

"Bourbon," the stranger told him. "You gents like to have one with me?"

Usually the guy who comes into a bar the last few minutes before closing has already been drinking pretty heavy; he's been put out of a place that shuts up early and he's looking for that last drink that's suddenly become so important. This guy was an exception; he was cold sober. About thirty, which makes him a few years younger than me and maybe twenty years younger than Sam, he was neatly dressed and had an air of sharpness that seemed out of place this time of night.

"Thanks," I told him. "I could use another beer."

Sam poured the stranger's whiskey, drew my beer and then got himself a glass of vermouth, which is the only stuff I've ever seen Sam drink.

Sam said, *"Prosit."*

The stranger said, *"Skoal."*

I said, "Here's how," and we all started working on our drinks.

I said something about the weather and they both agreed and everybody lapsed into silence. After a minute or two, the stranger started looking at the tabloid I'd discarded.

Finally he laughed and said, "Did you see this item about the old lady that socked some punk who was trying to hold up her liquor store? She slugged him with a bottle of Scotch."

Sam said, "Did it break the bottle? She would've saved money if she'd used something cheaper."

"Every once in a while you read something like that," I said. "That old doll must be a terror. I'd hate to be her old man."

The stranger finished off his drink and ordered another. Sam glanced up at the clock, saw we had time, and said this one was on him. I had another beer.

"The guy was an amateur," the stranger said. "If he'd had any sense, he wouldn't have tried anything on the old lady."

"Hell," I said, "How'd he know, when he pulled the gun on her, that she was going to haul off and conk him with a bottle? It was just one of life's little surprises."

"He should've sized her up before pulling the caper. If he'd taken his time, he could've seen she was the type that'd blow her top and start screaming, or throwing things or some such. Five minutes of analyzing her character and he would've seen he'd better go somewhere else."

"Maybe you're right," Sam said argumentatively, "but how would he go about analyzing her character in just the few minutes time he'd have? He couldn't hang around the store very long or it'd look suspicious and she'd be calling for the cops."

"You wouldn't need very long," the stranger told him. "You can size a person up in a just a few minutes by the way they walk and talk and by their gestures—that sort of stuff."

I grinned. "Okay. Size me up. If you were analyzing my character, would you go ahead and stick me up or not?"

He smiled back. "Sure I would. You're the easy-going type. Even if you had much money on you, and you probably never have, you wouldn't think it was worth taking a chance on getting yourself killed."

Sam grunted, "That sounds like Jerry, all right. How about me?"

The stranger flicked his hand almost disdainfully. "You're easy. I'd take a chance on you right off the bat. You'd be scared stiff at the first sight of a gun."

The old boy was irritated. "Where'd you get that idea?"

"It's the little things I watch," the stranger said. "Like the fact that you crook your little finger when you pick up your glass. A thing like that tells a lot."

Sam had been just about ready to take a sip from his vermouth. Sure enough, the little finger was crooked. It looked sort of ridiculous on the part of a big burly guy like Sam.

Sam snorted.

The easy-going smile left the stranger's face. He put his right hand in a pocket and brought out a snub-nosed revolver.

His voice was chilly now. "Let's try the experiment out," he said. "This is it. Fork it over, gents."

I said, "I'll be damned," and got my hands up in a hurry. "Take it easy, buddy—sometimes those things go off," I told him nervously.

He smiled a little, contemptuous smile at me and waggled the gun at Sam. "You too, big boy," he snapped. "Put 'em up."

Sam stood there, his two beefy red hands on the bar, and stared blankly at the gunman for a long moment. Finally he gave a deep sigh, and began to make his way around the end of the bar.

"Hold it," the stranger said sharply. "Get back to that cash register and—"

"In your hat," Sam said, coming toward him.

"Take it easy, Sam!" I warned him shrilly, expecting to hear the gun's roar at any split second.

But he kept advancing.

A muscle was twitching in the gunman's neck; his finger began to tighten on the trigger. "You're asking for it," he snarled.

"And over your ears," Sam said, and reached out suddenly and hit the guy sharply across the wrist with the edge of his hand. The gun dropped to the floor, and Sam stooped quickly and scooped it up with his left hand.

"Call a cop, Jerry," Sam told me softly, keeping the gunman covered. He made his way around the end of the bar again, and took his old place.

I went down to the other end of the room, where Sam has a pay phone booth, and shakily made the call.

By the time I came back I was boiling, I was so mad. "You conceited crackpot," I snapped at Sam. "Just because he said you'd be yellow in an emergency, you didn't have to show off like that."

The gunman had slumped back onto a stool, perspiration standing out heavily on his forehead. He started to say something, but then shut up.

Sam shrugged. "There wasn't any danger of his shooting. Any guy with enough brains to figure out that character analysis stunt before pulling his stickups has too much sense to kill a man. He wouldn't want to risk a murder rap. As it is, he'll only get sent up for a year or so."

He picked up his vermouth glass and finished his drink. I noticed that he stilled crooked his little finger. He saw my eyes on it and grinned wryly. He held it out so that I could see a small white scar running along the knuckle.

"Piece of shell fragment creased it back during the first war. Haven't been able to bend that finger since," he said.


## Questions for Students to Discuss

1. Explain why you do or don't see parallels between the knowledge practices and dispositions in the "Scholarship As Conversation" frame and the characters in this story.
2. The characters in Reynolds's story have a conversation about "sizing a character up." When sizing an issue up, experts understand that it may have more than one answer. In what ways did or didn't the stranger do this?
3. Scholarly conversations take place in many venues. This story, however, takes place in one venue, a bar. If the conversation took place in another venue (for example, a bank or airport) how might that venue impact the conversation?
4. Scholarly conversations occur over time. How much time passes in this story? Is there enough time for the characters to discuss,

debate, and enrich their understandings of personality analysis? Justify your answer.

5. The stranger shared the method he used to analyze a person's likelihood of resisting a holdup. To what degree did the other characters contribute to and build on the stranger's method and conclusion? Why is or isn't their level of participation important?

6. What is the moral of this story in terms of the "Scholarship As Conversation" frame?

# 6

# SEARCHING AS STRATEGIC EXPLORATION

Although it is tempting to think of research as a linear process (e.g., develop a question > generate keywords > search databases > analyze the results > write the conclusion), it is often not that straightforward or easy. One key to becoming an effective researcher is learning that the process is iterative and that you discover more as you go. An iterative process is repetitive. If you are conducting library research, for example, it might look more like this: formulate a question > generate keywords > search a database > analyze your search results > find new and better keywords > perform another round of searching in a different database with the new keywords > examine and compare the results in previous searches > change your original question. Each new round of searching leads to more questions and, hopefully, improvement of your ideas as well as the development of entirely new questions. So rather than a simple, straight, and steady process, research consists of forward, backward, and sideways movement with sudden lurches, pauses, and gaps.

In "The World Where Wishes Worked," Stephen Goldin provides us with a character—a fool—whose first attempts at searching do not provide adequate results. However, the fool persists in the face of search challenges and continues to repeat and modify his search. Although he exhibits mental flexibility and creativity, the result of his search and exploration is undesirable for most.

In Justin Case's story "Many Happy Returns," an elderly couple searches for people who will enable them to extend their lives. Pointing to the findings of an obscure mathematician, the couple relies on a serendipitous search technique to find the right people so that they can apply his theory. Their novice search strategies, secrecy, and unethical behavior raise questions about the nature and context of the search process.

"They're Made out of Meat" by Terry Bisson tells the story of extraterrestrials searching for sentient life in our part of the universe. When they encounter a sentient species that is fundamentally different from themselves, they use iterative questioning to make sense of their discovery. Although they reluctantly strain their mental flexibility, ultimately, they refuse to let their findings and exploration lead to new and progressive understandings about the nature of sentience.

These stories assist us with understanding the "Searching As Strategic Exploration" frame in textbox 6.1.

Textbox 6.1

**Searching As Strategic Exploration**

**Searching for information is often nonlinear and iterative, requiring the evaluation of a range of information sources and the mental flexibility to pursue alternate avenues as new understanding develops.**

The act of searching often begins with a question that directs the act of finding needed information. Encompassing inquiry, discovery, and serendipity, searching identifies both possible relevant sources as well as the means to access those sources. Experts realize that information searching is a contextualized, complex experience that affects and is affected by the cognitive, affective, and social dimensions of the searcher. Novice learners may search a limited set of resources, whereas experts may search more broadly and deeply to determine the most appropriate information within the project scope. Likewise, novice learners tend to use fewer search strategies, whereas experts select from various search strategies, depending on the sources, scope, and context of the information need.

**Knowledge Practices**

Learners who are developing their information literate abilities

- determine the initial scope of the task required to meet their information needs;
- identify interested parties, such as scholars, organizations, governments, and industries, which might produce information about a topic and then determine how to access that information;
- utilize divergent (e.g., brainstorming) and convergent (e.g., selecting the best source) thinking when searching;
- match information needs and search strategies to appropriate search tools;
- design and refine needs and search strategies as necessary based on search results;
- understand how information systems (i.e., collections of recorded information) are organized in order to access relevant information;
- use different types of searching language (e.g., controlled vocabulary, keywords, natural language) appropriately;
- manage searching processes and results effectively.

**Dispositions**

Learners who are developing their information literate abilities

- exhibit mental flexibility and creativity;
- understand that first attempts at searching do not always produce adequate results;
- realize that information sources vary greatly in content and format and have varying relevance and value depending on the needs and nature of the search;
- seek guidance from experts, such as librarians, researchers, and professionals;
- recognize the value of browsing and other serendipitous methods of information gathering;
- persist in the face of search challenges and know when they have enough information to complete the information task.

## THE WORLD WHERE WISHES WORKED BY STEPHEN GOLDIN

There once was a world where wishes worked.

It was a pleasant enough place, I suppose, and the people were certainly happy. There was no hunger in this world, for a man had only to wish for food to have it appear before him. Clothing and shelter were equally easy to obtain. Envy was unknown there—if another person had something that seemed interesting, it was only a wish away from anyone else. There was neither age nor need. The people lived simple lives, devoted to beauty and the gentle sciences. The days were a pleasant blur of quiet activity.

And in this world, there was a fool.

Just the one.

It was enough.

The fool looked about him one day, and saw that everything was the same. Beautiful people doing beautiful things amid the beautiful scenery. He walked away from the others, down to a private little dell beside a lily pond, overhung by graceful willows and scented with spring fragrance. He wondered what things would be like if something new or different were to be. And so he concocted a foolish scheme.

"I wish," he said, "that I had something that nobody had ever had before."

Only a fool could have made a wish like this, for he left the object of his desire completely unspecified. As a result, he instantly came down with Disease, which had hitherto been unknown. His eyes went rheumy and his nose went runny. His head ached and his knees wobbled. Chills ran up and down his spine.

"I dod't like this," he said. "Dot at all. I wish to cadcel my last wish." And he immediately felt well again.

"That was close," he sighed, as he sat down on a large rock beside the pond. "The trouble is that I don't think before I say things. If I thought things out first, I wouldn't get into so much hot water. Therefore: I wish I would think more before I do any more wishing." And so it was.

However, being a fool he failed to spot the fallacy of his logic: namely, that a fool will think foolish thoughts, and no amount of foolish thinking will help him make wise wishes.

Thus deluded, he began to think of what his next wish should be. He did not even consider wishing for wealth, since such a thing was impossible in a world where everyone had anything. Material desires were too commonplace. "What I should wish for in order to satisfy this new restlessness of mine," he thought, "is the rarest of all commodities. I wish for love."

A frog jumped out of the lily pond and landed *squish* right in his lap. It looked up at him adoringly with big froggy eyes filled with tenderness, and croaked a gentle love call.

"Yuk!" exclaimed the fool, and he instinctively scooped up the frog and threw it as far from him as he could. The pathetic little creature merely croaked sorrowfully and started hopping back to the rock to be with its beloved. Quickly, the fool canceled his last wish and the frog, frightened, leaped back into the pond.

"That was a foolish wish," evaluated the fool. "Most of my wishes are foolish. Most of the things I say are foolish. What can I do to keep from saying foolish things?"

Had he not been a fool, he would simply have wished to say only wise things from then on. But, fool that he was, he said, "I know. I hereby wish not to say foolish things."

And so it was. However, since he was a fool, *anything* he could say would be foolish. Consequently, he now found that he could say nothing at all.

He became very frightened. He tried to speak, but nothing came out. He tried harder and harder, but all he accomplished was getting a sore throat. In a panic, he ran around the countryside looking for someone to help him, for, without the ability to speak, he could not undo that previous wish. But nobody was about, and the fool finally fell exhausted beside a footpath and started to sob silently.

Eventually, a friend came along the path and found him. "Hello," said the friend.

The fool moved his mouth, but no sound escaped.

"I don't believe I heard you," the friend replied politely.

The fool tried again, still with no success.

"I am really not in the mood for charades," said the friend, becoming annoyed over the fool's behavior. "If you can't be more considerate, I'll just leave." And he turned to go.

The fool sank to his knees, grabbed his friend's clothing, tugged at it, and gesticulated wildly. "I wish you'd tell me what the matter was," said the friend.

"I made a wish that I not say anything foolish, and suddenly I found that I couldn't say anything," the fool told him.

"Well, then, that explains it. I am sorry to say it, my friend, but you are a fool, and anything you say is likely to be foolish. You should stay away from wishes like that. I suppose you want me to release you from that wish."

The fool nodded vigorously.

"Very well. I wish you could speak again."

"Oh, thank you, thank you."

"Just be careful of what you say in the future, because wishes come true automatically, no matter how foolish they are." And the friend left.

The fool sat down to think some more. His friend had been right—anything he was likely to say would be foolish, and his wishes would automatically come true. If that were so (and it was), he would always be in trouble. He could remain safe by not saying anything—but he had just tried that and hadn't liked it at all. The more he thought, the worse the problem became. There seemed to be no acceptable way he could fit into the system.

Then suddenly the answer came to him. Why not change the system to fit himself?

"I wish," he said, "that wishes did not automatically come true."

Things are tough all over.

## Questions for Students to Discuss

1. In Goldin's story, each wish is a search for something the fool desires. Each desire rested on an information need. To what extent did the fool recognize and think about the information he needed before his first wish? How did this affect the results of his first wish? What might the fool have done differently to improve the outcome of his first wish?

2. "The World Where Wishes Worked" raises an interesting question about improving one's searching. When describing the main character's wish not to say foolish things, the author writes "since he was a fool, anything he could say would be foolish." Do you

agree with this? What are the consequences of this principle for becoming a better searcher?

3. In what ways does your search strategy for school assignments resemble the fool's search strategy for his wishes?

4. At one point in the story, the fool can say nothing at all. In a panic, he seeks guidance from a friend. Instead of a friend, though, are there any experts with whom the fool may have consulted? What about when you do research? At what point, if any, do you seek guidance from a friend? How about an expert such as a professor or librarian? Why do (or don't) you like seeking guidance in your searching?

5. The majority of those living in "The World Where Wishes Worked" appear content with the system. Does this make the fool's desire to change the world wrong? By analogy, say, for example, the majority of students at your school are happy with finding their answers to life and school assignments using Google or Wikipedia. Whatever answer they wish for appears on Google or Wikipedia. Why do or don't you feel that a teacher who attempts to change this by requiring students to use multiple sources and to seek guidance from experts is wrong (or at least misguided and doomed to failure)?

6. The "Searching As Strategic Exploration" frame states "searching for information is often nonlinear and iterative, requiring the evaluation of a range of information sources and the mental flexibility to pursue alternate avenues as new understanding develops." In what ways does and doesn't this story illustrate these ideas? Justify your answer by showing how the fool does or doesn't do this.

## *MANY HAPPY RETURNS* BY JUSTIN CASE

The house was an old one on an old road, miles from anywhere, but the freshly painted sign by its driveway—TOURISTS' REST—was as reassuring as a cleric's smile of welcome.

"Let's," Grace Martin said, squeezing her husband's hand. "There's no telling what we might find!"

Their car was already bulging with antiques collected in six states, but Tom Martin didn't care. He had just acquired his M.A., a teaching job at a highly regarded prep school, and a beautiful bride. "Done," he agreed without hesitation.

The warped and weathered door creaked open as they wriggled from the car. A man as old as they had expected, with a crown of white hair glowing in the dusk, limped down the rickety steps to greet them. An equally old woman, doll-dainty, smiled and nodded in the doorway.

It was the woman who escorted the newlyweds to their upstairs room. "Our name is Wiggin," she said, "but please call me Anna. And when you've freshened up, do come down for tea."

Grace Martin became enthusiastic about the massive four-poster bed while her husband irreverently bounced on it and pronounced it comfortable. They "freshened up" by lamplight and went downstairs to a dim parlor filled with antiques and the smell of age.

Anna Wiggin poured tea into fine old cups, and her husband Jasper, in reply to Grace Martin's question, said in a cracked voice, "No, we do not collect antiques. Not really. We have just acquired these things as we needed them."

"You are only just married, you two," Anna said with her smile. "I can always tell."

"Five days," Grace admitted.

"You are very young," Jasper said.

"Not so young. I'm twenty-two. Tom is twenty-four."

The old man moved his head up and down as if to say he had made a guess and the guess was correct. He did not say how old he and Anna were. He did remark, "I am a little older than my wife, also," then sipped his tea and added, "You must tell Anna your birthdays. She will read your futures."

"By our birthdays?" Grace Martin said.

"Oh, yes."

"How can you do that, Mrs. Wiggin?"

"I can do it." The doll-woman leaned closer, nodding and nodding. "When were you born, my dear?"

"May eleventh."

"It won't work, you know," Tom Martin said with a grin. "She—" Then puzzled by the old woman's expression, he was silent.

Jasper rose from his chair and placed his hands on his wife's frail shoulders. Though all but transparent in the lamplight, the hands were strong and long-fingered. "Now, Anna," he said softly, "do not be excited."

Grace Martin sent a half-frightened glance at her husband and said, "Is there something special about that date?"

"It is Anna's birthday also."

"Oh, how nice! We *are* special, then, aren't we?"

"Don't go putting on airs," Tom Martin chided. "You're forgetting—"

"Now, darling, don't spoil it."

"I will get some more tea," the old man said. "Fresh cups, too. We must have a toast."

The others were joking about the birthday when he returned from the kitchen with a tray. Placing four full cups on the table, he sat down again. The lamplight splashed his shadow on a wall as he raised a hand and said, "To the day that gave us two such lovely ladies."

They laughed and drank.

"You see, my dear," the old man said to his wife, "it never fails."

"What never fails?" Tom Martin asked.

"Only yesterday Anna was saying we would have to leave this house and find another. So few travelers use this old road any more. And even with many guests we sometimes wait years, of course."

"Wait for what?" Tom said.

"They have to have the same birthday, you see."

Tom nodded solemnly. It was past the old folks' bedtime, he supposed. When you were that old, a break with custom could make the mind a bit fuzzy. "Well, of course—" He started to rise. Grace and he had had a long day too, more than three hundred miles of driving.

"Wait, please," Jasper Wiggin said. "It is only fair that you understand."

With a tolerant smile Tom sank down again.

"There is a mathematical master plan, you see," the old man said. "Each day so many people are born, so many die. The plan insures a balance."

"Really?" Tom suppressed a yawn.

"I can simplify it for you, I think, if you will pay close attention. Each date—that is to say, each eleventh of May or ninth of June or sixth of December and so forth—is a compartment in time. Now suppose a thousand people are born today, to take their place with all the thousands born on this date in previous years. If the plan were perfect, all those born today would live exactly a year longer than those born one year ago, and so on. You follow me?"

"Uh-huh," Tom said sleepily.

"But the plan is not perfect. There is a thinning out through sickness and accidents—there has been from the beginning—and as a consequence, some of those born today will die before the expiration date, and others will live beyond it to maintain the balance."

"Sure," Tom mumbled.

"Each time compartment in each of the time zones is controlled this way. Life moves according to mathematics, just as the stars do."

"Remarkable," Tom said. Across the table his wife Grace was practically asleep. "What about the normal increase in population?"

"Oh, that's accounted for. So are wars, plagues, and things of that sort. If we had more time, I could make it all quite clear."

"You discovered this yourself, Mr. Wiggin?"

"Oh, no. There was a man from Europe staying with us one summer—a mathematical genius named Marek Dziok. Not in this house, of course; we have moved many times since then. Dziok had an accident—he was very old, and one night he fell down the stairs, poor man—but before he died, he took us into his confidence."

"I see."

"You don't believe me?" Jasper Wiggin said. "Dziok was writing a book—a philosophy based on his mathematics. He never finished it. But I have the manuscript. . . ." He left his chair and limped to a bookcase, from which he lifted out a thin, paper-bound sheaf of papers. "Perhaps you would like—but no, you won't have time." Shaking his head, he put the sheaf of pages back.

"I guess I'd better take my wife to bed," Tom Martin said. "She's asleep."

"Yes, it works faster on women."

"What works faster?"

"The powder."

"You mean you put something—" Staring at his wife, Tom placed his hands flat on the table and pushed himself erect. It required enormous effort. "You mean—"

"You haven't been listening, have you?" the old man complained sadly. "And I've tried so hard to explain. Your wife and mine share the same time compartment, don't you see? You know yourself by now that Anna and I are much older than people get to be *naturally*. There's only the one way to do it."

"By—by killing off—"

"Precisely."

"And you think you're going to kill *Grace*?"

"It's been nineteen years since that last one for Anna," the old man sighed. "Hasn't it, dear?"

The doll-woman nodded, "Jasper has been luckier. He had one eight years ago."

"You're crazy!" Tom Martin shouted. "Both of you, you're crazy! Grace, wake up! We're getting out of here!" But when he leaned across the table to shake his wife awake, his legs went limp. He collapsed onto his chair. His head fell on his hands.

After a moment he was able with terrible concentration to bring the faces of Jasper and Anna Wiggin into focus again. There was something he had to remember—something he or they had said earlier, or he should have said but hadn't. . . .

"It won't hurt, you know," the old man was saying sympathetically. "You'll both be asleep."

"Both . . . both . . ."

"Oh, yes. We'll have to kill you too, of course. Otherwise, you'd tell."

"Wait," Tom whispered. The room was filling with shadows now. "Wait. . . ."

"But it won't be a waste, your dying. Somebody in *your* compartment will benefit, you know. Somebody with your birthday."

"Birthday," Tom repeated. That was it—birthday. "You're wrong about Grace—about—her—birthday." He made a supreme effort to get the words out before it was too late. "I tried—to tell you. She wasn't born May eleventh—"

"Oh, come now, Mr. Martin," the old man said sadly.

"No, no, it's true! She was born May eleventh in *Manila*. The Philippines. Her father taught—taught college there. Different—time—zone. Don't you see? A whole—day—different—"

The room went dark. In the darkness, though, he thought he heard the old woman begin to weep, and was sure he heard the old man saying, "Now, now, Anna, don't do that. There will be another one before too long."

Then nothing . . .

He was in the big four-poster bed when a shaft of sunlight wakened him. His wife lay asleep at his side. Their clothes were neatly folded on chairs.

Tom yawned and sat up. His wife opened her eyes and said, "Hi."

"You know something? I don't remember going to bed last night," Tom said.

"Neither do I."

"I don't remember getting undressed or folding my clothes like that. Grace"—he was frowning now—"I *never* fold my clothes. You know that."

"All I remember," she said with a yawn, "is getting sleepy at the table." She looked at her watch. "Anyway, we'd better be moving. It's after nine."

When they were ready to go they walked downstairs together, Tom carrying their suitcases. Anna Wiggin came from the parlor to greet them. "Did you sleep well?" she asked, peering into their faces.

"I'll say we did," Tom said.

"You were both so tired," Anna said, nodding. "Won't you have breakfast before you go?"

They said no, thanks, they were late as it was, and Tom took out his wallet to pay for their night's lodging. Anna said wait, please, she would get her husband, he was out in the field. So Tom and Grace Martin went to their car with the suitcases and Tom went back into the house alone.

It came back to him when he walked into the parlor and saw the table and tea service and the extra cups. The extra cups! At first it was fuzzy and confused; then it sharpened and he remembered everything—just as Grace had remembered everything up to the time of *her* falling asleep.

He snatched the sheaf of papers from the bookcase. It was indeed a manuscript, handwritten and yellowed with age. Its title was *The Mathematics of Life* and its author was Marek Dziok.

Under the author's name, in a different hand, was written: *Born 1613. Died (by accident) 1802.*

There was a sound of footsteps in the kitchen. Tom thrust the manuscript inside his shirt and quickly stepped away from the bookcase.

"You know, I'm still sleepy," his wife said later as their car purred along a parkway. "It must have been that house. They were nice old people, though, weren't they?"

"Remarkable," Tom said.

"I wonder how old they really are."

Tom did not answer. He had already finished his figuring and now he was thinking of the pilfered manuscript inside his shirt. That, too, was remarkable. With the information it contained, a man could live a long time.

Of course, it was all pretty weird and sinister. Nevertheless . . .

In spite of himself, he began to think about birthdays—his wife's and his own.

## Questions for Students to Discuss

1. The "Searching As Strategic Exploration" frame states that "the act of searching often begins with a question that directs the act of finding needed information." In this story, the Wiggins are searching. What is the question they ask the Martins that begins and directs the act of finding the information they need?

2. The Wiggins have been searching for years. However, do you think they have broadened their strategy or become better searchers over time? What might they do to improve their search strategy to find people who share their birthdays?

3. Anna and Jasper Wiggin search people. In this story, they searched Tom and Grace Martin. In what ways is searching a human being both similar to and different from searching a database, the Internet, or any collection of information? Before answering, consider online dating. In what ways is searching for a potential husband or wife online similar to or different from asking them questions on a face-to-face date? How would you

change your search strategy to match these different information sources?

4. The Wiggins asked the Martins a simple question: "When were you born?" Considering their actual information need, though, was this an effective question? What other questions should the Wiggins have asked? Why do you think they neglected to ask these questions?

5. When the Wiggins came across the secret to life extension in Marek Dziok's work, were they intentionally searching for it? What are some conclusions you can draw about the nature of searching and discovery?

6. What is the morale of this story in term of searching?

## THEY'RE MADE OUT OF MEAT BY TERRY BISSON

"They're made out of meat."

"Meat?"

"Meat. They're made out of meat."

"Meat?"

"There's no doubt about it. We picked up several from different parts of the planet, took them aboard our recon vessels, and probed them all the way through. They're completely meat."

"That's impossible. What about the radio signals? The messages to the stars?"

"They use the radio waves to talk, but the signals don't come from them. The signals come from machines."

"So who made the machines? That's who we want to contact."

"*They* made the machines. That's what I'm trying to tell you. Meat made the machines."

"That's ridiculous. How can meat make a machine? You're asking me to believe in sentient meat."

"I'm not asking you, I'm telling you. These creatures are the only sentient race in that sector and they're made out of meat."

"Maybe they're like the orfolei. You know, a carbon-based intelligence that goes through a meat stage."

"Nope. They're born meat and they die meat. We studied them for several of their life spans, which didn't take long. Do you have any idea what's the life span of meat?"

"Spare me. Okay, maybe they're only part meat. You know, like the weddilei. A meat head with an electron plasma brain inside."

"Nope. We thought of that, since they do have meat heads, like the weddilei. But I told you, we probed them. They're meat all the way through."

"No brain?"

"Oh, there's a brain all right. It's just that the brain is *made out of meat*! That's what I've been trying to tell you."

"So . . . what does the thinking?"

"You're not understanding, are you? You're refusing to deal with what I'm telling you. The brain does the thinking. The meat."

"Thinking meat! You're asking me to believe in thinking meat!"

"Yes, thinking meat! Conscious meat! Loving meat. Dreaming meat. The meat is the whole deal! Are you beginning to get the picture or do I have to start all over?"

"Omigod. You're serious then. They're made out of meat."

"Thank you. Finally. Yes. They are indeed made out of meat. And they've been trying to get in touch with us for almost a hundred of their years."

"Omigod. So what does this meat have in mind?"

"First it wants to talk to us. Then I imagine it wants to explore the Universe, contact other sentiences, swap ideas and information. The usual."

"We're supposed to talk to meat."

"That's the idea. That's the message they're sending out by radio. 'Hello. Anyone out there. Anybody home.' That sort of thing."

"They actually do talk, then. They use words, ideas, concepts?"

"Oh, yes. Except they do it with meat."

"I thought you just told me they used radio."

"They do, but what do you think is *on* the radio? Meat sounds. You know how when you slap or flap meat, it makes a noise? They talk by flapping their meat at each other. They can even sing by squirting air through their meat."

"Omigod. Singing meat. This is altogether too much. So what do you advise?"

"Officially or unofficially?"

"Both."

"Officially, we are required to contact, welcome and log in any and all sentient races or multibeings in this quadrant of the Universe, without prejudice, fear or favor. Unofficially, I advise that we erase the records and forget the whole thing."

"I was hoping you would say that."

"It seems harsh, but there is a limit. Do we really want to make contact with meat?"

"I agree one hundred percent. What's there to say? 'Hello, meat. How's it going?' But will this work? How many planets are we dealing with here?"

"Just one. They can travel to other planets in special meat containers, but they can't live on them. And being meat, they can only travel through C space. Which limits them to the speed of light and makes the possibility of their ever making contact pretty slim. Infinitesimal, in fact."

"So we just pretend there's no one home in the Universe."

"That's it."

"Cruel. But you said it yourself, who wants to meet meat? And the ones who have been aboard our vessels, the ones you probed? You're sure they won't remember?"

"They'll be considered crackpots if they do. We went into their heads and smoothed out their meat so that we're just a dream to them."

"A dream to meat! How strangely appropriate, that we should be meat's dream."

"And we marked the entire sector *unoccupied*."

"Good. Agreed, officially and unofficially. Case closed. Any others? Anyone interesting on that side of the galaxy?"

"Yes, a rather shy but sweet hydrogen core cluster intelligence in a class nine star in G445 zone. Was in contact two galactic rotations ago, wants to be friendly again."

"They always come around."

"And why not? Imagine how unbearably, how unutterably cold the Universe would be if one were all alone. . . ."

## Questions for Students to Discuss

1. The "Searching As Strategic Exploration" frame argues that the act of searching requires "mental flexibility to pursue alternate avenues as new understanding develops." Why do or don't you believe that the extraterrestrials in this story displayed these behaviors? What should or shouldn't the extraterrestrials have done to become better searchers and critical thinkers?

2. Because the extraterrestrials found beings made of intelligent flesh disgusting and contact with them awkward, they decided to erase the records of their discovery and not make contact. In effect, they acted as if the meat did not exist. To what extent do you see parallels between the extraterrestrials' behavior and a researcher who skips print books because they are inconvenient? Due to the inconvenience of going to the book stacks and getting a print book, some students act as if that information does not exist and never examine the ideas contained in these books. To

what extent is the student's avoidance of paper sources similar in spirit to the extraterrestrials' avoidance of sentient beings made of meat?

3. The extraterrestrials conclude that the existence of sentient beings made of meat is limited to one planet. Why do or don't you think they have enough information to complete their search and arrive at this conclusion?

4. What was the purpose of the aliens' search for sentient life in this part of the universe? How did this purpose shape how they did or didn't search for life as well as their final conclusion about the existence of intelligent meat?

5. At its best, searching is not a repetitive mechanical task but a deeply reflexive process. Ideally it sparks insight and enables searchers to broaden their knowledge and understanding about a topic. To what degree and why do you agree or disagree that the extraterrestrials in this story developed their insights and understandings of sentient life? If you had to rewrite the end of the story, what would you change and why?

6. When it comes to searching for information, what is the moral of this story?

# ABOUT THE AUTHORS

**David J. Brier** is a social sciences librarian at the University of Hawaii at Manoa and is currently the chair of the business, humanities, and social sciences department. He has a PhD in political science and a master's in public administration from the University of Hawaii at Manoa along with a master's of library science from the University of Michigan. He is the coauthor (along with his colleague, Vicky Lebbin) of numerous articles on information literacy. Their latest article, "Learning Information Literacy through Drawing," explores their ongoing interest in alternative teaching methods for information literacy instruction. His current research focus is on multisensory information literacy.

**Vickery Kaye Lebbin** is a social sciences librarian at the University of Hawaii at Manoa and is currently the public services division head. She holds a master's in library science from the University of Michigan and a master's in communication from the University of Hawaii at Manoa. Vickery is a former winner of the Association of College and Research Library Instruction Section's Innovation Award, honoring librarians who have unique approaches to information literacy instruction, and the Hawaii Library Association's Distinguished Librarian Award. Her publications include numerous journal articles, book chapters, and reviews on a variety of library instruction and information literacy topics.